ENCOUNTERS FOR UNITY

edited by

G. R. Evans
Lorelei F. Fuchs S.A.
Diane C. Kessler

The Canterbury Press
Norwich

Copyright © The Canterbury Press Norwich 1995

First published 1995 by The Canterbury Press Norwich
(a publishing imprint of Hymns Ancient & Modern Limited
a registered charity)
St Mary's Works, St Mary's Plain,
Norwich, Norfolk, NR3 3BH

A catalogue record for this book is available
from the British Library

ISBN 1–85311–096–5

*Typeset by Waveney Studios
Diss, Norfolk
and printed and bound in Great Britain by
St Edmundsbury Press Limited
Bury St Edmunds, Suffolk*

Preface

This book was born of encounter, of a chance meeting of its
editors, and a conversation from which came the idea that
it might be valuable to draw together the ecumenical experiences of some of the leading figures of the last few
decades. We thought it would also be timely. A number of
our contributors were in at the beginning of the events they
describe. Their generations hold in their collective memory
the flavour of the excitement of the early years of the World
Council of Churches and of the period after the Second
Vatican Council when churches began to talk to each other
with a renewed hope of unity. There has been a newness
about the ecumenical experience for them, a freshness of
hope, a pioneering dimension.

This is a book about the ecumenical experience as it looks
from the inside of the Christian world. Although one or
two of our contributors have also had experience of the
dialogues between the great world faiths, that is not our
primary subject here, because interfaith relations have a different purpose. For Christian ecumenism the goal is the
recovery of the unity in Christ which lies at the very foundation of the Christian faith. So what happens to people in
that search has a character which is special to that purpose.

Most ecumenists can recall an encounter or experience
which was decisive for their own ecumenical commitment
and formation, or which they perceive to have been for
someone else a pointer or a marker on an ecumenical journey. Tiny events grow and have long-term results. Bridges
are formed through personal encounter in Christian experience between the intimate, human, particular and the universal. Sometimes these personal bridges have institutional
implications. Ecumenical friendships can be a seedbed for
ecclesial growth. That is the kind of thing we asked our contributors to report for us. They have done it with openness,
honesty and often with humour.

Each contributor was asked to provide a concluding
prayer for the unity of the Church. We offer these for pri-

vate and group use, because prayer and spiritual ecumenism are central in responding to Christ's own prayer for unity.

We have made every effort to be inclusive, and to invite contributors representing a spread of geographic diversity, denominational balance, men and women, lay and ordained, of various racial and ethnic backgrounds. But we recognise that there are many more whose stories could be told here. We hope that this book will stimulate others to share their experiences, to witness to what they have seen and learned, and so to inspire new generations to take up the torch of ecumenical endeavour.

The book is intended to appeal to a wide general readership. It will have practical uses as starting-point material for meetings and discussion-groups, and provide texts to be read as opening meditations at the beginning of ecumenical gatherings, followed by prayer together. It may also have a role in devotional use, leading individual readers from reflection to prayer.

To help in the use of the texts we have borrowed a device much used by Christians in the first millenium and a half of Christian history, and taken out 'sentences' for discussion and personal reflection. The Latin *sententiae* means 'opinions'. Not all our contributors agree; but their views testify to the significance of ecumenical encounters in their own ecumenical formation and the way understanding of the profound unity of all Christians grows from it. Users of this book are taking part in the same common process .

Much of what our contributors have to say concerns this process which has come to be called 'ecumenical formation'. This must happen to separated communities, too, if unity is to become a reality. The churches also need 'ecumenical formation'. Thus, in our concluding chapter, we have attempted to draw some institutional lessons for the future from the raw data of these stories. We hope that in this way these texts will spur further reflection and action by churches to give renewed attention to their own communities' ecumenical formation.

Contents

v

Introduction

Personal journeys

We asked our contributors to tell us about themselves, about what has happened to them. We received stories of personal transformation. A number of themes emerged again and again. They are a good place to begin in giving an account of what 'ecumenical formation' means because they represent the natural patterns of the process.

Some of our contributors first had their ecumenical perceptions transformed by encounter with a living tradition different from their own. E. Glenn Hinson describes how he and his American Southern Baptist students went with 'defenses up' to visit a Roman Catholic monastery. 'All the Protestant histories we had read assured us that monasteries were at best relics of a bygone era and at worst wholly irrelevant to intelligent modern Christians'. They met Thomas Merton, for whom prayer was simply his vocation. Here was an ecumenical apostle who brought others to an insight into his own tradition. For Maximilian Mizzi the encounter which held a surprise about another tradition came when he happened to see two friars in Franciscan habits in Assisi. He discovered them to be Anglican Franciscans. 'I never heard of that before,' he comments. It taught him that a single Christian Tradition could persist in two separated communities with their own special traditions.

One significant result of that understanding for our ecumenists turned out to be that it gave them a deeper sense of the character of their own traditions. David Taylor comments on how necessary it is for ecumenists to be thoroughly grounded in their own traditions. Turid Karlsen Seim, who had a very thorough early traditioning in one confessional pattern, certainly found that. It is noticeable in these pages that those from each tradition tend to express similar insights. The realisation that different communities have different strengths and contribute as parts to the whole strengthens not weakens ecumenical commitment. It is relevant here that ecumenists do not as a rule 'change horses'. A Roman Catholic who has seen into the depths of the Evangelical tradition in Anglicanism (Tillard) has not become an Anglican; a Baptist who has seen the reality of the tradition of prayer in Roman Catholic monasticism (Hinson) has not become a Roman Catholic. They have stayed where they were in one sense, but in another they have become citizens of a greater city, the whole City of God. It has become their mission to bring the separated churches together in that living city of the one Church. They realize that all of us are drawn to the fullness of Christ's Church, which is Christ's before it is ours.

The perception of the underlying community in different traditions does not necessarily remove the sense of separateness all at once. Falconer points out that prejudices have to be unlearned. These pages seem to show that some of the biggest leaps of mutual understanding needed here have been between Orthodoxy and the Western traditions (where there has been a good deal of mutual ignorance); between the West and the churches of the the 'two-thirds world' (where there has been imperfect mutual respect); between Protestant and Roman Catholic (where there were long-standing hostilities).

All sorts of barriers operate internally, keeping Christians apart for reasons which sometimes lie very deep. There is frequently fear; there are anxieties which, as Mizzi found, can at last be set aside in ecumenical encounter. For some of our contributors the defining ecumenical experience has been the overcoming of a sense of alienation. Each felt, from a different vantage-point, a sense of disadvantaged or unappreciated 'otherness', in which there was an element of resentment to be overcome. This is a particular aspect of reconciliation which has proved ecumenically very important.

Paulos Mar Gregorios found the World Council of Churches at first 'too Western and too Protestant'. But two weeks in direct contact with it in Geneva began to show him that it was stimulating to exchange views with other kinds of Christians. At Yale he found his teachers all Protestants, who seemed to him to understand little of his tradition; the same tendency proved to be a problem at Oxford. It was the Third Assembly of the World Council of Churches at New Delhi in 1961 that made the difference. For this ecumenist it was the discovery that other Christians wanted to hear what he had to say in his Bible Studies on Ezekiel which overcame his sense of his tradition's being ignored by others.

Choan-Seng Song also began by feeling a cultural 'outsider'. He observes that after the Second World War, 'that ecumenical voice, which the World Council of Churches embodied, was heard mostly in Europe and North America'. But 'echoes of it reached Asia and other remote parts of the world known as the Third World'. Those echoes were enlarging for him because they created an awareness 'of a world Christian community beyond the missionary agencies that represented the churches in Europe and North America'. This created a cultural awareness both of 'Christianity' as a whole and of non-Christian cultures as they were experienced locally. The whole process altered mindsets and vantage-points.

Margrethe Brown has experienced the problems of overcoming alienation from both sides. She has found, as a woman, that she had to 'struggle to be included as a member of the community'. But she also saw, as she became acquainted with people of the 'Third World', their culture, economic plight and faiths, that there were 'cultural gifts and values' from which she had been cut off by her own limited cultural heritage. She has come to see herself as a 'learner' and to hold that 'our relationships never may exclude anyone merely who is 'different'. Others have found that the discovery of something in common which is central makes multicultural encounter possible in surprising combinations.

One of the results of overcoming a sense of alienation which our contributors celebrate with the greatest enthusiasm is the realisation that they have been liberated. Three of our Lutherans, two Europeans and an American, speak powerfully about this. For Günther Gassmann, as a young Christian in post-war Europe, living in a part of Germany under communist rule, the realisation that being a Christian means belonging to a world-wide community was a liberation from what he came to see as a political prison. The insight into the Christian implications came sideways, out of a sense of increasing constraint in a young life. But it proved to be the determining vision for a life's work. William Rusch too stresses the unexpectedness of the ecumenical realisation. He saw a similar opening-up of wider horizons in his own life as he gradually came to understand his confessional tradition in a context of 'the greater Church'. Both say that they found themselves changed and committed where they did not expect to be committed. They grew able to see on a grander scale and consequently to embrace a larger vision and hope for the Church. Margrethe Brown, born in Denmark and living later in the USA, also had 'the freeing experience that the world was bigger, and that in that world a faith was offered which sustained life.' For her, too, the ecumenical movement opened eyes and ears to the richness and diversity of human life, suffered and enjoyed, to be shared.'

Liberation may come quickly or slowly. Most of our contributors speak of the long, slow growth of their ecumenical development. They comment that ecumenists are made not born. Norman Young stresses the need for persistence and patience; there needs to be a slow a growing together out of which something new emerges.

But despite this consciousness of growth and process many of our contributors recognise defining moments, key points in the process when something had an impact upon them so powerful that they have never forgotten it. These are exciting, and they stick in the mind. Avery Post gives a list of such moments in his own life, which are still vivid and powerful for him. David Taylor was excited by a piece of writing. Alan Falconer, too, had the 'eureka' experience.

4

Sometimes the transformation is recognised by those to whom it has happened as a conversion experience. Turid Karlsen Seim says in so many words that 'for a Norwegian Lutheran of my generation to grow into ecumenical commitment is almost a conversion'. She grew up in a post-war Norwegian society of almost total homogeneity of 'devoted Lutheran confessionalism'; with a 'lack of awareness about the presence of other Christian communities in the country'.

Norman Young speaks of transformation, 'a process of change, of growing together out of which something new emerges', as he experienced it in the forming of the Uniting Church in Australia. For Alan Falconer the concept of 'transformation' even goes beyond that of 'conversion'. It is more than a radical change towards a new commitment and identity. It is 'a radical change of perspective in which some newly gained cognition brings about a changed way of understanding'. In his view the most important point is that it does not require a rejection or negation of the past or of previously held values. There is only gain and nothing is lost.

Our writers have an awareness of being changed by the journey of understanding and experience on which they are engaged, of the revolutionising of their viewpoints as they learn to see with other people's eyes. They have the 'freedom of the city' in the sense that they are drawn to dwell in friendship and harmony with all its citizens and see things as they do.

So our contributors report their sense of enlargement, the expansion of vision which makes them world-citizens. They find that does not diminish but enhances the richness of their local church life for them. It also heals. Their collective experience seems to show the lasting character of the changes they experienced which made them ecumenists. That would argue for the accuracy of the view of Alan Falconer and Turid Karlsen Seim that the ecumenical 'transformation' is very closely akin to the 'conversion' experience.

But conversion is never the end of the story. It is the beginning of a process of growth, in which there is always some element of healing. That too has been consciously present in our contributors' experiences. Avery Post describes growing up with a natural ecumenical awareness bred of his encounters from childhood in a religiously heterogenous community. It was always natural to him to think in terms of 'a very big, ecumenical God'. For him, as for Günther Gassmann and William Rusch, the characteristic effect of ecumenical awareness was a liberation into a larger world. But he adds another dimension from his experience of divorce within his family. That taught him at first hand about brokenness and the need for healing and reconciliation.

Emmanuel Sullivan's parents grew up in a divided Northern Ireland. His mother was a Protestant, his father a Roman Catholic. His mother had responded with a heroic tolerance to the experience of having her own father 'spat upon in Belfast because he had been mistakenly taken for a Catholic', a tolerance which she taught her son. From her he, like our earlier writers, learned that 'the grandeur of God and the greatness of God far exceeds the limitations and expectations we impose on God in our hearts and minds – and in our churches'. And he learned it by means of the mending of brokenness which his mother achieved, her own practice of reconciliation within the microcosm of her ecumenical family.

Both at the stages of coming to see what ecumenism means and why it is important, and during the long working out of its implications in a life, personal influence has been important. Here we come back to the primary ecumenical experience of 'encounter'. Several of our contributors have been won for or confirmed in their ecumenical commitment by others who have been for them 'ecumenical apostles'. Dean Freiday stresses that 'we should never lose sight of the fact that the lives and witness of twelve Apostles changed the world'. John Pobee has learnt to argue that 'personalities make ecumenism real'. Freiday emphasises the way in which an individual can make a group effort work. For Rusch, as for many of our contributors, teachers were important. Sometimes individuals perform an 'apostolic' function for one another. That seems to have been so in the case of the remarkable friendship of the Anglican Evangelical Julian Charley and the Roman Catholic Dominican Jean Tillard. We are seeing here in close-up and from within the kind of experience we can now only glimpse in the 'apostolate' of such earlier twentieth-century ecumenical figures as N. Söderblom (partly responsible for the success of 'life and work') and the 'Malines team' which included Cardinal D. J. Mercier, J. A. Robinson, W. H. Frere, C. Gore, B. J. Kidd, P. Batiffol, theologians of the Second Vatican Council. Our contributors clearly see the ecumenical endeavour as an apostolic task in the fullest sense of the word. They go out into the world for themselves and for others. There is a consciousness of being on pilgrimage, of travelling purposefully in this wider world. They experience a calling and a sending.

The apostolate has always been both universal and local. Paulos Mar Gregorios sees that 'the movement gains momentum at the local level'; 'churches and people at the local level have become highly active and creative'.

One profoundly important aspect of the 'locality' is the need to see ecumenical encounters happening at grassroots level, growing vigorously in each place. Maximilian Mizzi sees 'grassroot level ecumenism' as 'of the utmost importance'. 'It would be very helpful,' he says, if this is encouraged and fostered.' It was obvious to Choan-Seng Song that there was a need for a comprehensive review of Christian theological education, that there was an attempt to develop a 'Christian theology indigenous to Asia'. That has reversed roles, he argues, so that 'an ecumenical body such as the World Council of Churches now has much more to learn from theological developments in Asia and elsewhere than the latter from the former'. Alan Falconer speaks of communicating what one has learned ecumenically to others in one's own tradition. So the theological educational task for ecumenism has to learn to understand 'local' in all these and other ways.

Our contributors comment on the inadequacy of institutional approaches and the importance of the work of the Spirit in their own ecumenical journeys. The personal has mattered to them most in their own lives. Yet, as Emmanuel Sullivan stresses, 'we are shaped by the ministries we engage in' and it is of its essence that ministry takes place in community.

Our contributors are full of hope, the unexpectedness, the heightening, the excitement of the experience they have had. As Douglas Brown puts it,' if the twin foci of our existence are God and his world, as they were for Jesus, then the ecumenical nature of our life is given, it is unavoidable. The Church finds its place and its nature as an instrument, something which offers itself in the hope of being useful for the Kingdom, and it should become transparent in the process. Perhaps then our divisions would become less important, and might even shrivel away'.

The background

The novelty of much of today's ecumenical experience cannot be overemphasised. In previous centuries there have been many attempts at mending the divides in Christendom. Almost without exception, these have failed. Recognising the other person, the other church, as truly Christ's, seeing the task as having the kind of absolute imperative from which there is no withdrawal, are matters of inward experience as much as of intellectual position-taking and commitment and formal action.

The Council of Florence, which was held in the mid-fifteenth century to try to reunite the Orthodox and Roman Catholic communities, had mixed motivation. The Greeks needed the military help of the West in resisting Turkish invasion. A Decree of Union was signed in 1439, after conscientious bilateral dialogue over points of disagreement. But the Orthodox synods, most of whose members had not been present, and who did not feel that they could 'own' what had been agreed, could not ratify the Decree.

The Council of Trent in the later sixteenth century was

the result of some decades of attempts to call a General Council together to deal with the problems which were now dividing the Church in the West. But by the time it was held the divisions were deep, and it was impossible for all Christians to meet on a basis of equality and mutual acceptance. What was now at issue was the absorption of what were seen as 'dissident' communities by persuading them to 'return' to the Church. We could multiply examples of failures.

It is possible, however, by looking at the story of what has happened ecumenically in recent generations, to see from the outside how the conditions have been created in which our contributors were able to meet the very different experiences they did. By the late nineteenth century Christian missions had spread throughout most of the world. They had been denominational at the outset. But newly-converted Christians found it difficult to understand why, if they were all preaching the same Christ, Methodist and Anglican and Roman Catholic and other missionaries were not at one with each other. The way in which this awkward question led to the new insights of the World Missionary Conference of 1910 in Edinburgh is well-known. The Conference set about fostering cooperation among Missionary Societies. In the same period, the World Student Christian Federation grew out of a Student Christian Movement from the late nineteenth century. This tried to bring young people together from a wide range of churches for study-groups and camps. The idea was that they should learn to bear a common witness in the world. Some of the earliest twentieth century ecumenists were influenced by this movement.

These partly 'institutional' shifts reflected a growing sense that Christians made nonsense of their faith if they preached the gospel in opposition to one another and if they did not seek to bear a single witness.

Alongside these broad-based alterations of perception and priority ran the efforts of individuals with vision who were beginning to approach the task of uniting the Church from another direction, A well-known example is one unofficial forerunner of later bilateral dialogue. Between 1921 and 1925 conversations were held at Malines between Anglican and Roman Catholic theologians. Lord Halifax, himself a layman, had taken the initiative in bringing these about, but after the first meeting the Bishop of Rome and the Archbishop of Canterbury gave the exercise their blessing. A good deal of agreement was secured, but the results met with suspicion in communities to which all this was something unprecedented, and old hostilities were still fresh. In the 'old world' of entrenched division, the ground in which the seed could grow was still unprepared. One thing this experience showed was how unevenly the ground was then cultivated ecumenically. The Anglican Lambeth Conferences had been speaking positively about 'reunion' from their beginning in 1867, but on the whole without including the Roman Catholic Church on an equal footing in their plans with other churches. So talks could tend to produce agreements unevenly welcomed because of the sheer unfamiliarity of the attempt in certain contexts. The sense of discomfort, even outrage at the existence of division among Christians which was driving things in missionary contexts was not uniformly felt throughout the Christian world.

Another unevenness has been of a different sort. During its twentieth-century history systematic and organised ecumenism has been conscious of a tension between the perceived need for Christians to work together in the world to do practical good, and the need for them to recognise themselves as one body of Christ in one faith, to be visibly one Body of Christ. The 'life and work' aspects of the early twentieth century ecumenical movement were concerned with the relationship between Christian faith and social concerns. Nathan Söderblom, a Swedish Lutheran (1866-1931), had argued that if Christians did not allow their doctrinal differences to interfere, they could work together in practical Christian service straight away. There was an important Conference on these issues at Stockholm in 1925.

At Oxford, 1937, this branch of the movement began to lean towards the eventual union of 'Life and Work' with 'Faith and Order' in an attempt to mend divisions on the matters which were continuing to keep the churches apart. The Faith and Order movement itself had been especially concerned with the unity of the churches. Its Conference at Lausanne in 1927 was followed by another at Edinburgh in 1937, which also began to move towards uniting with Life and Work in what became the World Council of Churches in 1948. Within the WCC the priorities of 'peace and justice' (the old 'life and work'), and those of 'faith and order' still often appear to pull in different directions in more recent ecumenical history, and it seems that they reflect two faces of ecumenical concern which must always be to some degree in tension, at least in terms of the demand they make upon limited human energies. But even if they produce tensions as far as structures, funds and energies are concerned, they must ultimately find ways to work together in the one *ecclesia* which the conciliar movement of today's ecumenical Councils of Churches seeks to reflect.

The World Council of Churches was formally constituted in Amsterdam in 1948. It described itself as a 'fellowship of churches which accept our Lord Jesus Christ as God and Saviour'.

'Here at Amsterdam we have committed ourselves afresh to Him, and have covenanted with one another in constituting this World Council of Churches. We intend to stay together. We call upon Christian congregations everywhere to endorse and fulfil this covenant in their relations one with another. In thankfulness to God we commit the future to him' (*Message* of the Amsterdam Assembly)

The World Council of Churches never sought to be itself the future united Church. It respected the autonomy of the ecclesial bodies which joined it. They did not include all the churches at the outset. More but not all have since joined, and it remains the most comprehensive body of Christian communities. Above all, it tries to foster encounters in which mutual knowledge and understanding might grow toward unity:

> 'The purpose of the World Council of Churches is not to negotiate unions between churches, which can only be done by the churches themselves acting on their own initiative, but to bring the Churches into living contact with one another and to promote the study and discussion of the issues of church unity' (Central Committee of WCC, Toronto, 1950).

This seemed from the early years a sound practical way of encouraging the 'ecumenical formation' of the member communities, though it grew more ambitious as the vision expanded:

> 'As we seek to draw closer to Christ we come closer to one another' (Third World Conference on Faith and Order, Lund, 1952).

> 'We must together seek the fullness of Christian unity. We need for this purpose every member of the Christian family ... Our brethren in Christ are given to us, not chosen by us' (New Delhi Assembly, 1961).

But it was clear that something would also be required, if unity was to come about, and that it might be sacrificial:

> 'When churches, in their actual historical situations, reach a point of readiness and a time of decision, then their witnessing may require obedience unto death. They may then have to be prepared to offer up some of their accustomed, inherited forms of life in uniting with other churches without complete certainty as to all that will emerge from the step of faith' (Evanston Assembly, 1954).

Important, too, in those early years, was an awareness of the need to keep a lively sense of the focal points provided by the local churches in the local scene:

> 'The place where the development of the common life in Christ is most clearly tested is the local situation, where believers live and work. There the achievements and the frustrations are most deeply felt: but there too the challenge is most often avoided ... we are still far from being together

in all those ways in which ... we might be' (New Delhi Assembly, 1961).

That brings us to the period when some of our older contributors began to become involved. They lived through the transformation brought about by the ecclesiological opening-up of the Second Vatican Council, with its recognition of the true ecclesiality of other Christian communities. On that recognition it became possible to build dialogues undertaken in a spirit of true equality between the partners, with real mutuality of commitment. The setting-up of the first Anglican-Roman Catholic International Commission is a notable example, with numerous other bilateral dialogues soon accompanying it in its efforts. The great multilateral achievement of the 1980s was the Baptism, Eucharist and Ministry 'Lima' text of the World Council of Churches.

Often, the official dialogues, formal committee work and the discussions which result, seem abstract, abstruse and far removed from the interests and concerns of the average churchgoer. Yet if the participants in these formal ecumenical structures are asked to 'tell their stories', a liveliness and energy shows through, and helps us comprehend the fundamentals at the root of the formal discussions.

That is one reason why we asked some of them, and others who have been active ecumenists in other ways, to contribute to this volume. Personal story-telling can be an instrument of the ecumenical evangelism which began to grow at last out of the separated missionary efforts of the nineteenth century.

Note on spelling
We have retained English or American spelling as our contributors have used it.

Douglas Brown

SSM (Society of the Sacred Mission), Director of The Anglican Centre in Rome. *Anglican.*

POSSIBILITIES of ecumenical activity have opened up before me throughout my life, and in every case, where the door was open, it seemed natural and right to go through it. It might be thought that belonging to a religious society and theological college on the top of Mount Lofty in South Australia, a place remote from the City of Adelaide in the 1950s, would be a poor way to be ecumenical. The same might be said of our House at Kelham in the 1960s. But ecumenical life came to meet me there. Members of religious Orders are not closely involved in the clerical structures of a denomination – unless we have the misfortune to be called to 'high office'. We were at all times the object of streams of curious visitors (and they were objects of curiosity to us), and of course we were bound to be conscious of our multitudinous *confrères* in the Roman Catholic Church.

Although we were saddled with a stiffly 'High Church' tradition at that time, yet we knew we were rather peculiar in our church, and so we were ready to go new ways. In this time I was fortunate in having, as a teacher and a friend, Gabriel Hebert, SSM, a pioneer among ecumenists. In Australia at that time we were a little free from our tradition because the churches there were all finding their roots in the new nation, so that none of the churches were quite so caught up in their history as the parent bodies in Europe were. As members of a religious community we were a little outside the ordinary life of the Anglican church and looking on. Sometimes we were a little supercilious too, I think.

Later, I found myself back in Perth as a University chaplain. It seemed natural for the three of us who set up the first chaplaincy there to act together as a team. We emphasised the difference between being 'Chaplain to the

Anglicans at the University' and being 'Anglican Chaplain' (or 'Catholic' or 'Uniting' to the University). It was the sense of being able to serve all of those students, teaching staff, management, gardeners – we felt we had functions within the whole community, and I think that they came to recognise us as a kind of 'servant trinity'.

From there in the early seventies I was brought into an ordinary parish in Canberra, the Australian national capital. It was not quite an ordinary parish, since it had petitioned the bishop to be closed. Perhaps its very weakness was an attraction to us as we set up our first 'parochial priory' in Australia. But the attempt to cope with establishing the work of the Church in a modern city soon pitched us into the question of ecumenism once again. Under the guidance of the Anglican bishop, Cecil Warren, the Woden Churches Centres sprang into being. It seemed very adventurous to go to financiers for a million dollar loan, to build a five storey office building in the middle of Woden, one of the city centres of Canberra, and to have a permanent chapel and a large meeting room-cum-church on the top floor. Our congregation used it every Sunday – it became our parish church. It was owned by all of the main-line churches who together formed a Company. It was also used by all kinds of groups, especially by the Telephone Samaritans. The Church and the city came together at the natural centre, on the Woden Plaza. The physical building was easy, but it was much harder to evolve a programme, a way of using this facility, and I do not think that we ever fully realised its potential.

A different kind of ecumenical experience came when I had to move from Canberra to Adelaide again in the late seventies. This time it happened in the field of theological education. For someone as secular minded as myself, theological colleges had very obvious shortcomings. In Adelaide meetings had been going on for some time before I got there, under the chairmanship of Siegfried Hebart, the head of Luther Seminary. In quite a short time the six theological colleges (but alas! not the Lutherans, blocked by their national synod) came together to form the teaching faculty for a theological degree offered in the Flinders University. One thing I liked about the set-up was the requirement that each student had to do a third of her studies in non-theological subjects. At first they were closely watched by the University teaching staff to see whether they could cope with 'real' studies through the mist of superstition. But they triumphed because they were highly motivated. They also gained enormously through contact with one another from different church traditions – and not only because the women students were keen to get to know those potential celibates from the seminary. We teachers also gained by contact with one another, and by being able to specialise in our work. I think I shall always look back at the formation of the Adelaide College of Divinity and its association with Flinders University as a major achievement in the life of the Church in Australia.

In more recent times ecumenical work has become part of my everyday life. First, in Bucharest, where the warmth of welcome of the Orthodox fraternity was always astonishing. 'But the others, they are too proud!' said a professor in the Theological Institute. And perhaps that is it, after the oppression and impoverishment of the communist régime, they are ready to grasp our hand if we reach out to them. But also, we learn from them the depth of a faith which can survive under persecution. In Rome, of course, my work at the Anglican Centre is more 'Church-oriented', in the sense that here we have to represent the Anglican Communion. My Anglicanism, previously, was something rather taken for granted, and now has to be taken out and scrutinised. Official churchdom is all around us. It takes an effort sometimes to reach the human being under the soutane. But working here with the Vatican and the churches in Italy I am grateful that the focus of theological work is not on the internal arrangement of the church, but upon the world and its needs. Here we are all grateful inheritors of the insights of the Second Vatican Council, and I feel that my own 'worldliness', often so distressing to the more 'spiritual' members of my Community, has recognition and acceptance.

Thinking over my experience in ecumenical matters has led me to the idea that ecumenism has come easily to me, perhaps, because I have never been closely caught up with the organisation of the Anglican church; in fact, I don't think I am a 'churchly' person. People interest me, and ideas, and science, and history and nature, but not church services. In the same way, ecumenism is important to me because it brings people together, and it is overcoming some of the historic barriers; but on the other hand meetings of Councils of Churches and the official side of ecumenism leave me cold. That is why I have been impressed by some of the unofficial groups who work for ecumenism in Italy – something I have not known elsewhere. I welcome the fact that more 'unofficial' groups are forming in Britain and America – this is where important thinking and understanding might take place.

If there is any overall meaning to this pilgrimage, perhaps that is it. If the twin foci of our existence are God and his world, as they were for Jesus, then the ecumenical nature of our life is given, it is unavoidable. The Church finds its place and its nature as an instrument, something which offers itself in the hope of being useful for the Kingdom, and it becomes transparent in the process. Perhaps then our divisions would become less important, and might even shrivel away.

PRAYER

Lead us, Lord, beyond all we can know or imagine,
beyond the limits of our group, race or country. Lead
us to trust in your grace and love your life-giving
Sprit. Lead us into your gift of unity which
transcends all of our littleness. Lead us to Christ
our Lord, through whom we ask this.

Sentences for discussion

Peace and justice
If the twin foci of our existence are God and his world, as they were for Jesus, then the ecumenical nature of our life is given, it is unavoidable.

Perseverance
We learn from them the depth of a faith which can survive under persecution.

Margrethe B. J. Brown

formerly Associate of the New York State Council of Churches, New York, USA. *Presbyterian Church (USA).*

BROADENING involvement in the life of the Church and continuing renewal of faith through encounters with those who are in some way different from myself and who offered to share their faith, have characterized my growing commitment to the whole Church.

The parochial life of faith in a Lutheran Parish in Denmark, and my early experiences in the Student Christian Movement – first as a high school student, later through ties with the wider Christian community in Europe and beyond – set a direction which gave form to the working out of much of my life. Later, when I was living in the USA, the constant question why the churches appeared divided in spite of the prayer of John 17. 20–24, that those given faith may be one in God, became one which I had to ask. I needed to ask it both of the denominations, and of colleagues within the ecumenical movement. Some found it difficult to hear when the question was asked by a woman.

Particular incidents and personal encounters made the initial enthusiasm stick.

First there was the freeing experience that the world was bigger, and that in that world a faith was offered which sustained life. The ecumenical movement opened my eyes and ears to the richness and diversity of human life, suffered and enjoyed, as something to be shared, given and received in the midst of a community, enormously diverse and rich, created by a loving God.

There were the friends in the Student Christian Movement who invited me to come along, to speak up in the Bible and mission study groups and to participate in the fun of week-ends in the country and summer camps and meetings. There were the leaders who dared to allow emerging leadership capacities to grow, be tested and expand, because they themselves were sufficiently rooted in God's faith not to be threatened. There were also the pro- fessors and pastors who opened up ever broader visions of faith, and ever greater opportunity for commitment. There were those who helped me understand that fear, guilt and isolation were foreign elements in a life in faith.

From my Lutheran background came the awareness that recognition of sin and forgiveness were not only for one- self but also for others, that others, regardless of their 'difference' were given life on the same terms as 'we' were, for God loved 'them' as well. People who gathered in Lund in 1952 spoke about the wholeness of God's Church while the gruelling and inhumane images of the Holocaust and World War II were still fresh on the backs of our eye- lids.

With faith based in an ever widening community, theo- logical studies made me question the division of the Lord's Table. My faith concluded that what God provided was more than formal expressions of doctrine had been able to say, and the table, albeit diversely presented, could never be privatized to exclude 'others'.

Such community-based faith also sustained a woman through the 1950s and 60s seeking acceptance as an equal among theological students, pastors and church leaders, virtually all of whom were male and most of whom never had questioned their own position of dominance in either personal or communal relationships. A 'retrospective' can- not separate the tracks of ecumenical formation from the emergence of a sense of a 'right to be and to question' which later years identified as a feminist claim. Similarly to the women who experienced the need for their own emancipa- tion, my ecumenical work experience cannot be separated from the struggle to be included as a member of the com- munity, with a set of experiences and expectations which were formed and shaped by the fact that I am a woman. If God could expect us to be one with those who at various times in history had fought us, was there any reason that women of faith should not celebrate the Lord's Supper?

The impact of particular historical and cultural developments upon human lives in community and the need to challenge their limitations, formed my ecumenical commitment. It also shaped my quest for acceptance of those commitments as the sexism in the Church and the world became personally evident to me. I came to see that the barriers of confessionalism and those of sexism are both rooted in historical constructs which demand revision in light of the prayer of John 17.

But ecumenical formation is not something with which one some day gets finished and done. The world is indeed without end. Along with the international ecumenical encounters came acquaintances with people of the 'Third World', their cultures, economic plight and faiths.

The challenge to rethink mission in line with more appropriate church-to-church relationships reformed my originally very traditional concept of white peoples' duty to provide the proper faith for the rest of the world (complete with evergreen Christmas trees with candles, even if the tropical night melted the candles before they could be lit). An acceptance of the relationship of faith to culture, and of the relativity of any culture to a variety of expressions of faith in God incarnate, now had to be incorporated into the basic commitment of faith in community.

New cultural gifts and values expanded the world that I previously had perceived merely as a North Atlantic one. However, I also saw the radical economic and social needs that were first created by white colonialism, and subsequently maintained by the neocolonialism of which my own existence is part. These factors forced us to review and reshape the earlier notion of the unity of the Church which was held by those in Lund, who spoke so strongly to the torn cultural fabric of post World War II Europe. Its relative cultural monotone makes it inadequate and the broader notions of wholeness which contributes to 'one world' offer a deeper understanding of what Jesus might have had in mind as John presented his original prayer in the language of the late Roman and Greek world of that time.

Further questions and new understandings have come
from conversations with people of other living faiths, along
with the surprising experience of a deepening of my own
faith where I learned about the faith of others. Here the
differences are deeper yet than social structures, languages,
cultures and economics. Yet the original realization, first
held within the traditional Lutheran notion of 'simul justus
et peccator',[1] says precisely that we – I – or you – remain
learners and our relationships may never exclude anyone
who is merely 'different'.

PRAYER

*May God's people be one as we are loved in the
divine mystery and unity of the Creator, the
Redeemer and the Sustainer.*

Sentences for discussion

Respect for others
We – I – or you – remain learners and ... our relationships
may never exclude anyone who is merely different.

Peace and justice
The challenge to rethink mission in line with more appropriate church-to-church relationships reformed my originally very traditional concept of the white peoples' duty to
provide the proper faith for the rest of the world.

Demolishing barriers
I came to see that the barriers of confessionalism and those
of sexism are both rooted in historical constructs which
demand revision in the light of the prayer of John 17.

NOTES
1. 'At the same time righteous and a sinner'.

Edward Idris Cassidy

Cardinal, and President of the Pontifical Council for Promoting Christian Unity. *Roman Catholic.*

TOWARDS the end of 1989, Pope John Paul II asked me to take over from His Eminence Cardinal Johannes Wille-brands as President of the Pontifical Council for Promoting Christian Unity. Though I had, in my position as Substitute (or Under-Secretary) of the Secretariat of State, given much thought to the nomination of a successor to Cardinal Wille-brands, I had never for a moment imagined that I might be asked to fill the huge vacancy that he would leave.

In the days following my appointment, my anxious thoughts naturally turned to those events in my life that might now help me to carry out my new responsibilities more effectively. On looking back, I could fortunately recall experiences that might well have sown the seeds for a pos-itive ministry in the field of ecumenical relations. The first of these was my own family background. For while my ancestors came from Ireland, some were from the north and strongly Presbyterian, while others came from the south and were deeply Roman Catholic.

One of my relatives on the Protestant side was a well-known barrister in Sydney, Australia – Sir Jack Cassidy. We were good friends, and he was pleased when I became an Archbishop in the Roman Catholic Church. When some of his friends learnt, however, that he had a cousin who was an Archbishop in the Roman Catholic Church, they found this hard to believe – and I suppose that some of my friends would have found it strange to think that a Presbyterian as well-known as Sir Jack might possibly have a relative in such a position within the Catholic Church. 'You see', a friend once said to me, 'your cousin kicks with the other foot!'

Another of these personal experiences came from my years as a seminarian in Australia. I referred to the following incident during the dinner which followed the installation of Dr Carey as Archbishop of Canterbury in April 1991. During my summer holidays as a seminarian of St Patrick's College, Manly, Australia I used to do some work in a large department store in Sydney. One year – probably 1945 or 1946 – I found working in the same section of the store two other theological students: one from the Anglican College at Morpeth, New South Wales, and the other a young Methodist. We got on famously – to the annoyance of our supervisor, who was a Jehovah's Witness. We had long discussions and quite a few arguments. What seems strange to me today is that while each one strongly defended his own tradition, the idea of Christian unity never entered our young heads. In fact, when my Methodist friend invited me to be present at his first sermon (at that time a truly ecumenical gesture), I had after much reflection to refuse with deep sorrow, since I believed that my presence might cause much difficulty both to him and myself. We have come a long way since then, and for this I am truly grateful.

Looking back now, I am convinced that despite the lack of any vision of Christian unity among Australian Christians in general during those years before the Second World War, our society was such that we were spared much of the bitterness that characterised Christian relationships in other parts of the world. If we did not exactly love one another, we did have good relations with our neighbours irrespective of their religion – and indeed we were often inspired by their Christian lives to live our own religion better.

After my ordination to the priesthood I spent just three years in parish ministry, before post-graduate studies in Rome, at the end of which I was invited to join the diplomatic service of the Holy See. The experience of being part of the Church in so many different regions of the world – for the diplomatic staff of the Holy See has much more to do with Church than state – has proved to be a great help to me in these past years in the Pontifical Council for Promoting Christian Unity. One of the important tasks of the Papal Representative, as defined in Canon Law (Canon 364, 6) is 'to cooperate with the Bishops in fostering suitable relationships between the Catholic Church and other churches or ecclesial communities ...'

I should like to recall just one event from those years. I was posted to the Nunciature In El Salvador from 1967 to 1969. In San Salvador, there was a church which sought to provide ministry for people of various Reformed traditions who did not have a church of their own in the capital. Services were in English, but it was not easy to find a minister who would accept the post or who would be acceptable for long to such a diverse group of parishioners. In their need, the community leaders sought to invite ministers from other churches in El Salvador to come from time to time for their Sunday worship. To my great surprise, I was asked to do this on one occasion and must certainly have been the first Roman Catholic priest – I was a Monsignor at the time – to lead the Sunday service and preach the sermon at a Protestant church in El Salvador. This was in the years immediately following the Second Vatican Council. Perhaps the Lord was already then showing me that I would not conclude my active ministry in the diplomatic service, as seemed certain at that time, but in the great task of promoting the unity of all Christians. The following is the prayer I offer as I seek to carry out to the best of my ability this task:

PRAYER

*Heavenly Father, we wish only to be faithful to the
task you have given us, of bringing together all those
who are your disciples into a real and perfect
communion in your Son Jesus Christ. Send us then
your Holy Spirit to guide us in this sublime mission
and open our hearts and mind to listen to what the
Spirit is saying to the churches. Free us from the
chains of unhappy past memories and from the
comfort of our division, so that we may all be one and
the world believe that you have sent your only Son
Jesus Christ to be Lord and Saviour of all creation.
Amen.*

Sentences for discussion

Getting the idea
I used to do some work in a large department store in
Sydney. One year – probably 1945 or 1946 – I found working in the same section of the store two other theological
students: one ... Anglican, and the other a young Methodist
... What seems strange to me today is that while each one
strongly defended his own tradition the idea of Christian
unity never entered our young heads.

Julian Charley

Member of the First and Second Anglican-Roman Catholic International Commissions (1970-91). *Anglican.*

PERHAPS some are born ecumenists; some undoubtedly have ecumenism thrust upon them. I most certainly belong to the latter category. Reared in an evangelical tradition where ecumenism was synonymous with unacceptable compromise, I had never taken more than an academic interest in the subject. Then, to my surprise, came the invitation from the Archbishop of Canterbury to be a member of what came to be known as ARCIC (the first Anglican-Roman Catholic International Commission). Ecumenism was problematic enough, but dialogue with Rome – that really was a leap into the lions' den. Moreover, I would be the only evangelical on the Commission. But I was encouraged to accept. If I refused, then there would be no evangelical voice there at all. It would serve no useful purpose to wring my hands with horror at any subsequent results, if I had spurned the original invitation. So it was that I found myself with some trepidation at St George's Windsor in January 1970.

It is an awesome experience to be placed in a position where a lot is expected of you and yet for which you feel markedly ill-equipped. A compensating factor was the general expectation of rather limited results to issue from the Commission. What inroads could we be expected to make into those intractable problems that had defied all previous attempts at resolution for four hundred years? One thing, however, soon became apparent – the 'learned footnote' mentality of the professional academic only too readily obscured the wood for the trees. At least that was not my problem!

As those early days progressed I found to my surprise that, when our discussions brought me elation or annoyance, similar emotions were shared by one of the Catholic

28

participants, Jean Tillard from Ottawa. Though emanating from such distinct theological stables, we began to discover a kindred spirit. Before too long we were being requested to undertake a substantial amount of drafting, a shared enterprise of genuinely dual authorship. A bridge was formed across the Anglican/Catholic divide from the quarter on the Anglican side whence it was least expected. Indeed I found in so many areas a greater affinity with the Roman Catholic Jean than I did with my Anglican colleagues. Such are the surprises ecumenism brings.

Bishop Alan Clark used to describe ARCIC I as a 'school for theologians' *(schola theologorum)*. It certainly was for me. Having to seek to penetrate into a very different theological tradition was both challenging and enriching. My evangelical convictions have not been altered, but they have been vastly enhanced and broadened. Gaps began to be filled, areas of superficiality were submitted to the deep furrows of the theological plough. It was an educational privilege in which we all shared. Along with this went an ever-deepening friendship and respect among the ARCIC members, which allowed complete candour without lasting animosity even at times of the most strenuous disagreement. In such a context the pain of not being able to communicate at one another's Eucharists is acutely felt.

Four years after that Windsor meeting I left theological college lecturing to return to parochial life. West Everton in Liverpool had a long history of Catholic/Protestant confrontation. The annual marches of the Orange Lodges[1] began and ended on our parish boundary. The bitter hostility between the two communities had done a lot of harm in the past. We set about healing the rift by cooperation with the local Catholic Church in various ways, a pattern warmly endorsed by almost all the local members of both communions. If the theological work of ARCIC was to succeed, it must eventually prove itself in places like Everton. It was my privileged position to be for the next sixteen years the only member of ARCIC who was at the same time a practising parish priest, an invaluable earthing for high-flying theology.

I think it was the Church of England Bishop David Sheppard whom I heard say of work towards the fuller expression of Christian unity, 'It's all a matter of obedience to Jesus Christ.' How blinkered I had once been not to see that! To have been involved in some small way in this work of ecumenism has been a privilege and an adventure that I would not have missed for the world.

PRAYER

*Our heavenly Father, we praise you for sending your
Son, the Prince of Peace, to heal all that disrupts the
harmony you intend for your creation. We thank you
that in Christ all human barriers are done away.
Grant to us, your people, grace through the Holy
Spirit so to be one in truth and love that the world
may believe. Amen.*

Sentences for discussion

Surprise
I found in so many areas a greater affinity with the Catholic Jean than I did with my Anglican colleagues. Such are the surprises ecumenism brings.

Calling
It is an awesome experience to be placed in a position where a lot is expected of you and yet for which you feel markedly ill-equipped.

Perhaps some are born ecumenists; some undoubtedly have ecumenism thrust upon them. It's all a matter of obedience to Jesus Christ.

The pain of separation
In such a context the pain of not being able to communicate at one another's Eucharists is acutely felt.

Grass-roots theology
If the theological work of ARCIC was to succeed, it must eventually prove itself in places like Everton.

NOTES

1. These are commemorative marches of the Orange Order, which was founded in 1795 to defend the cause of Protestantism in Ireland. They are occasions which heighten the tension between Protestant and Roman Catholic communities not only in Ireland but in cities such as Liverpool where many Irish settled in the past.

Choan-Seng Song

Professor of Theology and Asian Cultures, Pacific School of Religion and on the Doctoral Faculty of the Graduate Theological Union in Berkeley, California. *Reformed.*

THE FIRST thing that comes to my mind when I think of the ecumenical movement are those familiar words John the Baptist is reported to have said about Jesus and himself: 'He must increase, but I must decrease' (John 3.30). The story that follows is a personal account of how this applies in my experience in the ecumenical movement.

The ecumenical movement has, among other things, been an empowering movement. How much the world, not to say the Church, needed empowering in the aftermath of the Second World War! Nations and peoples were physically ravaged and spiritually devastated. For the world to rise like the phoenix from the ashes of horrendous ruins, to be open to the work of the Spirit in empowering the human spirit to recreate the history disrupted by the destructive powers released from the hidden recesses of humanity, there must be voices crying in the wilderness to turn despair into hope, and rekindle the vision for the future.

The ecumenical movement was one such voice. That ecumenical voice, which the World Council of Churches embodied, was heard mostly in Europe and North America. But the echoes of it reached Asia and other remote parts of the world known as the 'Third World'. It came in different forms and in a variety of ways. Those echoes enabled Christians and churches in Asia, for example, to be aware of a world Christian community beyond the missionary agencies that represented the churches in Europe and North America. These echoes also made them realize that they had to be part of Christ's body and not just an extension of Euro-American churches. Above all, these echoes compelled them to look at themselves in relation to the history and cultures, unrelated to Christianity, which they shared with the majority of their neighbors.

This was an ecumenical awakening that some of us in Asia, including myself, experienced in the early days of our ecumenical apprenticeship. In retrospect this kind of ecumenical enthusiasm was the privilege of a few 'enlightened' Christians, and it has remained so in most churches in Asia. For the great majority of Christians in Asia the ecumenical movement meant church leaders going overseas, particularly to Europe and North America, for meetings and conferences, bringing back ideas and information new and strange to them. In the past missionaries were the presence of the Western churches in Asia, but now on top of that presence 'ecumenical church leaders', both national and international, brought home the Western image of a world Church supposedly united in faith and action. The churches in Asia had been related to the churches in the West as 'receiving churches' through their mission agencies and missionaries. Now some of them also became churches receiving ecumenical 'visions', ideas and practices developed mostly in the West.

Most of us with young ecumenical minds inspired by the visions and activities of our ecumenical elders were eager to embrace the ecumenical movement. The Christian Church in a society under authoritarian rule needed, we thought, the strong support of a world Christian community. Christianity as a minority religion in a community of people of other faiths had to be united, we believed, in witness and practice. We saw that the Church divided into denominations was a disservice to the cause of the gospel. And we welcomed the emphasis of Christian responsibility for society and the world.

The churches in Asia had to have such an 'ecumenical blood transfusion' to be revitalized for God's mission in the world. The fact that the blood transfused was blood from the West did not matter much to us at that time. What was important for us was that the ecumenical movement was able to deliver what it advocated. And it did deliver a great deal. One of the things that are still vivid in my memory was the joint worship services held at the Roman Catholic cathedral and at the chapel of Tainan Theological Seminary, both in Tainan, my home town in Taiwan, in 1967. I remember on these occasions I preached a sermon entitled 'The Witness of Christian Unity'. Without the Ecumenical Council known as Vatican II those joint worship services could not have taken place. For myself, had I not been inspired by the ecumenical movement (although mostly second-hand at that time through senior ecumenical leaders), I would not have taken the initiative as the president of Tainan Theological College to bring about such ecumenical happenings (which I later came to know as 'local ecumenism'). Such local ecumenical events were few and far between in Taiwan and elsewhere in Asia in those days.

The ecumenical movement delivered more. A number of ecumenical projects funded by the World Council Churches got the churches involved in what was going on in society. Many of those projects were unfortunately to die a premature death, bringing chagrin to the project secretaries from Geneva and embarrassment to local church leaders. Still, I considered this to be a process of growing into ecumenical maturity on the part of those involved, whether from Geneva or from local constituencies.

In connection with the 'success' of the ecumenical movement in Asia, it is, in retrospect, not so much Church unity as the development of theological education that deserves special mention. And it is in the latter that the ecumenical movement in Asia can best be perceived to have decreased while indigenous theological movements have increased. I can speak about this with some degree of knowledge and experience because of my involvement in theological education most of my career. In the early days of the ecumenical movement the World Council of Churches, through the Faith and Order Commission, strove for Church unity in the sense of 'organic union'. Church unity still has to be a vision of Christians and churches in Asia, but due to reasons, historical, cultural, political and economic, it is no longer their primary concern.

Theological education in most Asian countries after World War II was in a shambles. In the pre-war era most theological schools were run by missionaries. They had left for their home countries because of the war and had not yet returned. School facilities were in a state of ill repair. Libraries were in a pathetic condition. Indigenous theological leadership was underdeveloped, to say the least. It was into this theological vacuum that the Theological Education Fund (TEF) entered. The TEF, an educational arm of the World Council of Churches, was the ecumenical movement at its best as far as putting theological education back on its track was concerned.

Through its dedicated staff, with experience, insights and vision in theological education, TEF, mobilizing ecumenical resources, came to Asia, as it did to the Pacific, Africa and Latin America, with very much-needed funds to rebuild the facilities, including libraries. But this is not all it did. What is more important, it brought creative ideas to stimulate, inspire, and develop local theological leadership. To be sure, most of these ideas of theological education and methods of implementing them were Western in form and content. But at that time how could anyone, even a most foresighted theological mind in Asia, have done otherwise? What TEF did was to contribute to the laying of the foundation on which theological efforts, ecumenical in nature and indigenous in substance, came to be developed later.

I am already ahead of the sequence of history that these brief reflections attempt to recapture. But looking at the ecumenical movement in the light of what has been happening in theological education, especially in the development of Christian theology indigenous to Asia, one thing becomes clear to me: the 'success' of the ecumenical movement in Asia through theological developments in the earlier times has diminished the role of the World Council of Churches in the continuing development of Christian theology in Asia today.

As a matter of fact the role has reversed. An ecumenical body such as the World Council of Churches now has much more to learn from theological developments in Asia and elsewhere than the latter from the former. How are we to deal with this reversal of roles? What does it mean for the World Council of Churches as it seeks to represent a world-wide community of its member churches? What is the direction the ecumenical movement should take in the next century? In a word, what is the destiny of the World Council of Churches as part of the ecumenical movement when the ethos, gravity and direction of the movement have shifted on account of the powerful dynamics of historical particularity and cultural-religious pluralism?

Of course a soul-searching question has to be asked at the present juncture of the history of the ecumenical movement, the question of whether we have ever achieved what I call ecumenical maturity. My own view is that dynamics of history and even some ecclesial power politics have so far held back the ecumenical movement from reaching maturity of love, understanding and statesmanship. This should be a matter of serious discussion within ecumenical circles. Implied in this observation is also my view that the 'success' of the ecumenical movement created the ecumenical situation today in which 'universal ecumenism' has decreased and 'local ecumenism' has increased, to paraphrase the quotation from John's Gospel I made at the beginning of my reflections.

To return to my narrative: armed with ecumenical enthusiasm and some experience of the ecumenical movement at the receiving end of it in Asia, I joined the World Council of Churches in Geneva, Switzerland, in 1973 as associate director of the Faith and Order Commission. I was very conscious of the fact that I was the first person to be on the staff of the Faith and Order Commission from the Third World since its inception in 1927. This fact, together with my involvement in the agenda of Faith and Order as time went on, made me ponder upon several anomalies and raised for me a number of awkward questions.

Here are some of those Faith and Order assertions and

the questions these assertions have raised for me. Although Church unity is something given in Jesus Christ, it is stressed, the truths enshrined in confessional traditions and doctrinal truths play an equally important role. Does this mean that the truths as we understand them and hand them down are as decisive as the unity given in Christ?

The unity of the Church, it is claimed, is the sign for the unity of humankind. The theological validity of such a claim apart, an urgent question is then: when are the churches going to achieve unity so that humankind may become united? And a not altogether hypothetical question follows: if the churches fail to achieve unity, is there no hope for humankind to become united in some way? This gives rise to an essential question: what kind of unity are the churches seeking? Organic union? Consensus in doctrinal matters? Agreement in the practice of faith, be it baptism, the eucharist, the ministry? Common witness not only in word but in action? Or unity in diversity, a concept that has come to replace the earlier visions of church unity?

Faith and Order questions such as these lead us to another. The World Council of Churches as a whole has always been acutely aware of this question but has not really confronted it theologically, and much less ecclesially. This is the question of the power that resides in the churches of different traditions and confessions, and especially the power that both symbolically and in actuality are represented by church hierarchies. I may be wrong, but all along I had the suspicion that the question of power 'was kept at a respectful distance' (*chin er yuan chi*, to use a Chinese expression), in Church union negotiations, because it was a very sensitive question and might jeopardize an already precarious road to some form of Church unity. But can a genuine unity of the churches be achieved without addressing it?

As a first Third World person to be on the Faith and Order staff, I felt like a stranger in the theological debates going on in earnest on traditional issues and problems. I began to ask myself whether these issues and questions were the issues and questions of the churches in Asia. A colleague of mine from India in the sub-unit on Dialogue with People of Other Faiths used to say to me that he had to deal not with his own questions but always with questions raised by the representatives and colleagues from the churches in the West. This frustrated him and I empathized with him. But I was determined to understand the traditions of Christianity as much as I could, and to expand and deepen whatever I had learned at various centers of theological learning in the West. I am grateful that Faith and Order offered me a great incentive to explore the legacies of Christian faith more deeply, especially those dimensions of legacies that created and perpetuated church division. Those endless theological debates in public and particularly in private with Faith and Order colleagues and Commission members were stimulating, but also often frustrating because I was fighting on the theological fronts defined by them and the perimeters of theology set by them.

In the course of time it gradually dawned on me that Faith and Order debates are not ecumenical debates until those of us from outside the West have theological substance of our own to put on the table for reflection and discussion. This, I think, is one of the most important things I have learned in those years of my involvement in the World Council of Churches through Faith and Order. This set me on the course of theological efforts in two directions besides those which were my responsibility within Faith and Order. I set out, on the one hand, to broaden my ecumenical experiences through contacts with colleagues and friends from different parts of the world; and on the other, to relearn church history through Christians and theologians from the other side of 'Christendom'. This was the beginning of a fascinating process of understanding Christian Church history in the context of world history. At the same time I began to engage myself in committing my theological reflections to writing – reflections informed, corrected, deepened and enriched by my study and exploration of Asian histories, cultures and religions.

During my past ten years I have been privileged to be a part of theological development in Asia. My involvement is intensive and rewarding. It confirms to be right what I did theologically during my tenure on the staff of Faith and Order. It also convinces me that with the increasing body of theological insights gained through the search for the theological meaning of life and history in Asia, we have to begin rewriting the history of Christianity in Asia not merely as a history of Christian mission but as a history of the mission of God in Asian history. We have, in fact, begun to develop our theological experiences of the life and ministry of Jesus in relation to our own stories as Asians and the stories of our Asian sisters and brothers in the past and today. What emerges will be a history of Christianity and its theology very different from what we are used to.

If this is the direction the theological movements in Asia are taking us, we have to ask whether the ecumenical movement, still represented by the World Council of Churches today, can still inspire us as it used to in earlier times. A question has to be raised whether the World Council of Churches as a fellowship of some three hundred member churches, still largely operating on the theological principles and assumptions defined by the traditions developed in the West, is in a position to chart a new course for those Christian churches which are now so diverse in theology and mission simply because of their being in diverse situations – situations radically different from those days when the World Council of Churches was inaugurated.

We also have to ask how the Christian churches are to play a constructive role together with other religious and cultural forces to mobilize the spiritual resources that would create moral strength to ensure life's meaningfulness in our everyday life within God's creation. This is an urgent theological and ethical question with which Christian churches have to grapple. Radical shifts in the Christian theological mind-set and its ecclesiastical orientation are needed for a task such as this. Is the World Council of

Churches, without fundamental changes in the ways it carries on its agenda and programmes, capable of being a catalytic force in this spiritual enterprise? This is another of the questions some of us in Asia are asking today about the ecumenical movement.

PRAYER

*O God, the Great Spirit of Wisdom, Love and
Creativity, grant us wisdom to understand what you
are doing in the world; inspire us with love to be
instruments of unity and peace in the contentious
religious world; and enable us to be part of your
creating a new heaven and a new earth in the old
creation that is passing away. Our prayer to you, O
God, is the prayer Jesus our Lord has taught us to
pray saying: Your will be done on earth as it is in
heaven. Amen.*

Sentences for Discussion

Two faces of power
The ecumenical movement has, among other things, been an empowering movement.

I had the suspicion that the question of power 'was kept at a respectful distance' ... in church union negotiations, because it was a very sensitive question and might jeopardize an already precarious road to some form of church unity. But can a genuine unity of the churches be achieved without addressing it ?

Belonging
I felt like a stranger in the theological debates going on in earnest on traditional issues and problems. I began to ask myself whether these issues and questions were the issues and questions of the churches in Asia.

Contributing
Faith and Order debates are not ecumenical debates until those of us from outside the West have theological substance of our own to put on the table for reflection and discussion'.

An ecumenical body such as the World Council of Churches now has much more to learn from theological developments in Asia and elsewhere than the latter from the former.

Martin H. Cressey

Principal of Westminster College, Cambridge, England. *United Reformed Church.*

THE WORD 'draft' has among its meanings 'select from larger body for special duty' and 'make preliminary version of document'. My ecumenical life began and has continued along those lines and I suppose will end when I can no longer draft in the second sense!

I had come to Coventry in the English Midlands, to take up the pastorate of St Columba's Presbyterian Church of England. Trained at Westminster College, Cambridge, I had spent a year there beyond my own course, as a tutor, with the duty of assisting the professors and the opportunity of continuing my own reading and reflection; now I was launched into the church life of a busy industrial city, still in 1959 in process of being rebuilt after the heavy air raids of the Second World War. It was already a place of ecumenical activity and ecumenical relationships; in particular a new Anglican cathedral had begun to rise in striking modern form beside the preserved ruins of the medieval one, and including in its building a Chapel of Unity, to be owned and used in the name of all the churches.

It was not long before I was drafted in the first sense, to be the first non-Anglican joint secretary of the council responsible for the Chapel of Unity. Almost immediately I discovered that those who drafted me had varied notions of how the chapel was to be used and of how the joint secretaries were meanwhile to be used to fulfill those notions. Wise senior friends began to teach me that drafting minutes for ecumenical committees is a skilled art. My next experience of being drafted was election to membership and then secretaryship of the committee appointed by the Congregational Church in England and Wales and the Presbyterian Church of England to prepare a plan of union, the union consummated in 1972 with the formation of the United

Reformed Church (joined in 1981 by the Re-Formed Association of Churches of Christ). Once again secretarial drafting was the skill needed.

Recently I preached at the thirtieth anniversary of the dedication of the Chapel of Unity; the United Reformed Church is now twenty-one years old. So I have 'come of age' in a generation span of ecumenical involvement.

My *curriculum vitae* lists quite a number of published articles, but the greater part of what I have written for the United Reformed Church, for the World Alliance of Reformed Churches, for the World Council of Churches Faith and Order Commission, is in files or printed texts where my work is as anonymous, though sometimes perhaps as detectable, as that of J, E, D and P in the documentary hypothesis on the composition of the Pentateuch – though I certainly am not claiming that it is inspired.

So for this symposium on ecumenical formation I offer some reflections on being drafted to draft.

In the first place it is not enough to be a volunteer. Of course, committees and conferences are delighted to have members volunteer to take minutes or prepare documents; but for ecumenical progress it is necessary that there be confidence in those who steer the process. It may begin, as it did with me, as confidence that the committee can control its young inexperienced secretary, but it has to grow into a confidence in someone whom they have freely chosen for this service and an assurance that the service is being rendered in a principled way. So drafters should be drafted, perhaps I may dare to say should be called. Having entered on a vocation, they have to learn some principles, even as I was taught by such skilled ecumenists as Eric Fenn, John Huxtable, Arthur Macarthur, David Paton (to name only a few) in the England of the 1960s.

Once in the secretary's chair, the drafter has to listen, to clarify, to include and to guard, in particular ways for these general functions.

Ecumenical listening is more than the courtesy of paying due attention to each speaker in a debate (though after writing out the draft at half past midnight, the basic courtesy has to be maintained in combat with sleep). There is a deeper listening which seeks to hear not only words but intentions. Often the listening drafter will have to call on a knowledge of the particular theological vocabulary, the liturgical customs, the social context of a speaker's church, not to mention the purely linguistic problems of listening to another language or to one's own language spoken with a different idiom. Having heard one speech, it is then necessary to notice whether responses have picked up the first speaker's intention or have perhaps misheard it, from the perspective of another church or tradition.

Given a set of notes of a conversation, the drafter now has to clarify the course of debate. It is rarely appropriate to give a verbatim account of an exchange between speakers; so a clear outline has to be produced of the issues under discussion, such that it strikes all the participants as a true representation of the contributions made, omitting mistakes, corrections, irrelevancies, but retaining what seem to the group as a whole to be the essentials (and here the drafter must give way).

At some point either the original group, or a wider circle in a conference, will hear or read the draft thus far brought to clarity. There will be a series of comments, some of them very strongly urged. Now the drafter has to include. The skills become more complex. There is a need for 'inclusiveness of language', removing male or female emphasis, or words offensive or demeaning to some persons; there is a need for an inclusiveness of theological perspectives, so that the draft does not presuppose a particular view of a doctrine; there is a need for an inclusiveness of concerns, so that examples are drawn from different parts of society or the world; and there is, of course, a need for an inclusiveness of comments, such that all who have commented on the earlier draft have a real sense that their point has been taken, even if not in the precise wording they suggested. With all that inclusiveness, something has to go out, lest the draft become intolerably lengthy; and to include involves excluding, often the most difficult achievement.

And so to the task of 'guarding'. By this I mean that a drafter, more than the participants in a particular debate, has to watch for the implications and the consequences of what is now being set down. The committee or the conference is not going to be grateful for accurate listening, clarifying and including if the ultimate readers discern that the text implies a heresy or points to some action which is ecumenically unacceptable. Some guarding can be done in the process of drafting, without the need to call attention to it (and perhaps involve the committee in hours more debate) but, if vital issues are at stake, then the drafter has to produce a referee's whistle as well as 'the pen of a ready writer' (or when things get really detailed, perhaps 'raiment of needlework').[1]

Ever since those first experiences as a minister in Coventry, amid friends, so many of whom have kept up their ecumenical work for a generation, I have been grateful to those who drafted me as a drafter and fostered in me the skills of that particular unspectacular but vital ecumenical calling.

PRAYER

Grant, O God of truth, that what is written for the reading of many may fully and accurately reproduce the views of those who engage in the quest for the visible unity of your church, having them say what they actually do say and in the way that they mean it, so that even those divided in faith may come to see that they are divided within the same faith, because they believe in the self-same Lord; for that Lord's sake we ask it. Amen.[2]

Sentences for discussion

The writer's calling
It is not enough to be a volunteer ... for ecumenical progress it is necessary that there be confidence in those who steer the process ... So drafters should be drafted, perhaps I may dare to say should be called.

Shared authorship
The greater part of what I have written ... is in files or printed texts where my work is as anonymous, though sometimes perhaps as detectable, as that of J,E,D, and P in the documentary hypothesis in the composition of the Pentateuch.

Listening
Ecumenical listening is more than the courtesy of paying due attention to each speaker in a debate ... There is a deeper listening which seeks to hear not only words but intentions.

NOTES

1. Cf. Psalm 45, verses 1 and 14, King James Version.
2. A prayer for ecumenical drafters, based on an exchange between Karl Barth and Hans Küng, cf. *Justification*, Hans Kung (reissued London, 1981), pp. xii and xxxix.

Paul A. Crow

President of the Council on Christian Unity of the Disciples of Christ, Vice-Moderator of the Faith and Order Commission, World Council of Churches, and Editor of the Journal *Midstream*. *Disciples of Christ.*

MY ECUMENICAL formation began in childhood as I heard and experienced the Gospel in the small First Christian Church (Disciples of Christ) in Lanett, Alabama, a textile town in the deep south. A succession of dedicated ministers and church school teachers impressed my young mind with the ecumenical faith. It was made clear that my baptism was not into the Disciples, or any other tradition, but into Christ. My membership was entry into the one Church of Jesus Christ. We were taught that the Lord's Supper is the Table of Christ's risen presence where all Christians gather to receive God's grace, be reconciled to God and to each other; and be sent into the world for service and witness. I was convinced that 'the plea' (vocation) of the Disciples of Christ and this congregation was to be a loving, reconciling church. It seemed simple and biblical.

Yet in those youthful days, I experienced the harsh divisions within the Church and society. First, there came the gradual consciousness of the reality that Alabama and the United States were a racially divided society. Black and white – both children of God – were separated by law, economics, culture and religion. The pain of racism bcame a nagging reality. Second, my deepest experience of the Church's disunity came at a happy personal moment when my church was rejected by the Roman Catholic Church. It was the occasion of my receiving the Eagle Scout award, to be presented during the Sunday service at my congregation. I invited my best friend Mug, a Roman Catholic of Italian descent, to be present and sit with my family during the presentation. I remember even now the deep pain and hurt when several days before the service Mug sadly told me he could not come into our church because his priest said to do so would be a mortal sin. The Disciples were separated from the true Church. At that moment I learned a divided Church hurts lives and relationships. Experiences of disunity – then and now – have motivated me and countless other Christians to work for the full reconciliation and *koiniona* (communion) of the Body of Christ.

During my high school and early university years I was drawn into the International Christian Youth fellowship – a formative programme for several generations of Disciples youth. In my years of participation, including a year as the president, watchful adult counsellors engaged me in the United Christian Youth Movement, which gathered young people from many traditions into a deeper understanding of the Christian faith and mission. Ecumenical youth conferences gave us friendship across the walls of separation – national, racial, denominational – and we heard world leaders such as Philip Potter, Hanns Lilje and D. T. Niles tell of the Christian vocation in a global ecumenical world.

In my senior year at the University of Alabama, God strangely changed the professional trajectory of a chemistry major and called him into the Christian ministry. Just as I was trying to understand the implications of this new vocation, another rather dramatic encounter took place that was to seal my life focus upon ecumenism. In this particular year the lecturer for Religious Emphasis Week, which annually gathered three thousand students for five days, was Dr Charles Clayton Morrison, a Disciples minister, founding editor of *The Christian Century*, and a leading ecumenist on the American scene. Since I was the student chairperson of REW, it was my responsibility to be Dr Morrison's host. Little did I know how transforming those days would be. Dr Morrison's lectures that week were from his book, *The Unfinished Reformation* (1953), a fiery denouncement of the evils of a divided Church, especially denominationalism; and an evangelical call to the glory and practical hope of the united Church for which Christ prayed. We were converted. In our final conversation during a spring day on that historic campus, Dr Morrison laid his hands on me and evoked a promise that wherever the ministry took me I would serve the unity of the Church. His invitation made a difference; his passion for Christian unity across the years has sustained one ecumenist through many uncertain waters.

This childlike vocation reached a new plateau during my seminary years. The College of the Bible (now Lexington Theological Seminary) in Kentucky was a theological and pastoral community with an ecumenical vision. The one Church of Jesus Christ pervaded the academic teaching – biblical studies, church history, homiletics, systematic theology, ethics and pastoral care. I sensed that the unity of the Church was an experience of the whole Gospel and a dimension of all ministries. Again, my ecumenical formation was shaped by persons and experiences that stretched me across the walls of separation. Dr Howard E. Short, my major professor in church history, tutored me through the divine-human encounter that shaped the faith and church institutions. We lived through the eras of patristic, medieval, Reformation, modern. Disciples history and theology applies to all eras. Amid the divisions and renewal movements across the centuries, we heard the struggles to become the one, holy, catholic and apostolic Church. Dr Short and other faculty also made sure that I experienced the wider ecumenical movement – appointing me secretary of a regional study group of the Greenwich Plan for Church Union, encouraging me to be part of a United Christian Youth Movement delegation to thirteen countries in the Caribbean and Latin America, guiding my BD thesis on 'The Nature of the Unity we Seek', pointing me to the Ecumenical Institute, Bossey, and mandating that I pursue a PhD degree in ecumenism and church history. Ecumenists who care about the next generation placed me in actual situations where the unity of the Church was experienced, struggled with and tested. I came to see that the ecumenical agenda is both theological and experiential, and the clue to leadership is affirming and relating both tasks.

In the summer between graduation from Lexington Seminary and the beginnings of my doctoral studies at Hartford (1957), Mary – my young bride – and I were invited to the North American Faith and Order Conference, at Oberlin, Ohio. She was the coordinator of the duplication of all documents; I was a steward – that honored preparatory experience for youth who want to learn about the ecumenical movement, especially Faith and Order, a shared part of our married life. The addresses and group work at Oberlin, focused on the theme 'The Nature of the Unity we Seek', offered the most comprehensive introduction to ecumenism the churches in the US had ever experienced. My BD thesis was both vindicated and made to seem inconsequential! A new development in our ecumenical formation was the many conversations and meals we had with exalted leaders who cared enough about the younger generation to listen to their queries and give them encouragement. I vividly remember time with W. A. Visser't Hooft, Georges Florovsky, Eugene Carson Blake, Paul S. Minear, James I. McCord, Albert C. Outler, Alexander Schmemann, Carlyle Marney, Samuel McCrea Cavert, Ronald E. Osbord, Mossie Wyker, Frances Maeda and Eleanor Kent Browne – the dynamic duo from the New York office of the WCC. Special was seeing Dr Short function in an ecumenical conference and walking arm in arm for the last time with C.C. Morrison. All of those persons eventually became friends and represent for me the communion of saints. I learned that authentic ecumenism requires leaders of deep faith and commitment to the Gospel who approach each other with respect and humility, eagerly learning from other Christian traditions, receiving the spiritual gifts and insights of each person and tradition as a sign of the Church universal.

A new stage of my ecumenical formation came in my years of graduate studies at Hartford Seminary Foundation. My key tutor now became Dr Robert S. Paul, Oxford D.Phil., former associate Director of the Ecumenical Instutie, Bossey, newly-appointed professor of modern Church History. The program on ecumenical studies he designed, along with the missionary resources of the Kennedy School of Mission make Hartford a unique place for ecumenical academic preparation and leadership development; seminars on the history of the modern ecumenical movement; controversial Faith and Order problems; biblical exegesis of unity passages; the witness of united and uniting churches in Asia, Africa, Latin America and Europe; ecclesiology; ministry and sacraments; Christian mission on six continents deepened my sense both of the God-given calling to unity and the human ambiguities of the churches, the ecumenical movement, and their institutions. My PhD dissertation on 'Unity and Diversity in the Faith and Order Movement', with Peter Berger and Nils Ehrenstrom as contrasting readers, equipped me for the changing dynamics and agenda that were looming ahead.

Those years were punctuated by overseas experiences, particularly in 1960, that brought me to the end of these 'early steps'. I was one of the American youthful delegates sent to the European Ecumenical Youth Assembly at Lausanne, Switzerland (similar conferences were held in North America, Asia and Latin America). There my vision of the Church was enlarged by friendships with young Bishop (later Metropolitan) Nikodim of the Russian Orthodox Church, Frère Roger Schutz of Taizé, Albert van den Huevel, Lewis Mudge, Nikos Nissiotis, Andrew Young, as well as other Lutheran, Reformed, Anglican, Orthodox, Methodist and Baptist young people. This conference was my first genuine encounter with the Orthodox church, and I became aware of the splendor of its liturgy and spirituality and the faithfulness of its teachings and mission in hostile contexts. We learned much from the addresses, but my deepest learning came from a crisis around the celebration of the Eucharist. In the midst of the enthusiasm of the Lausanne Conference a large number of delegates, mainly Protestants, called for a common celebration of the Lord's Supper in the Cathedral. This proposal was scandalous to the Orthodox, Roman Catholics, and some Anglo-Catholics.

The staff of the World Council of Churches and other planners of the Conference explained that such a common celebration could not be possible. The theological issues that divided the churches are not yet resolved; such intercommunion is forbidden by the canons and disciplines of several churches. Yet an unofficial eucharist did take place and we learned that more than enthusiasm is required to bring all Christians around the Eucharist together. Our celebration was a mixed sign of the disunity that burdens the churches and our yearning for wholeness. I learned that holy impatience is sometimes a gift of God, but cannot by itself bring the churches fully together in Christ. The processes of theological consensus-building and ecumenical praxis have to go hand in hand.

Just after the Lausanne youth conference a delegation of five youth delegates were sent to the Faith and Order Commission meeting in St Andrews, Scotland. There the final work was done on what came to be called the New Delhi Statement on Unity. We also listened to the reports of major Faith and Order studies moving toward the Fourth World Conference at Montreal. My vision of unity was enriched by Oliver Tompkins, Lesslie Newbigin, Russell Chandran, Lakdasa de Mel, Michael Ramsay, *et al*. My very first drafting assignment came when I was asked to present the report of the youth delegation. As I confessingly remember, we were a little haughty and judgemental towards our elders, but so have younger generations been from time immemorial.

These 'first steps'; created a calling and a journey for an Alabama boy who found his fullest faith and witness for the next thirty-five years in the official and unofficial ecumenical movement. The years brought unforgettable learning: the search for visible Christian unity is sustained by the Gospel of the triune God; unity comes to us as gift and struggle – both received in hope. From it all, I came to believe the vision of unity is worth the consecration of a life, my life.

PRAYER

Gracious God, source of all goodness and holiness, in Jesus Christ you have bound us in love to yourself. We thank you for the ministry of reconciling love given to us and the whole body of Christ. Forgive our acceptance of the divisions of the Church and our failure to carry your love into the world. Sanctify, renew and reconcile your people that we may be one people of peace and justice, and show forth the unity which the Spirit gives. In the name of our Redeemer and Reconciler. Amen.

Sentences for discussion

Ecumenical apostles
His invitation made a difference; his passion for Christian unity across the years has sustained one ecumenist through many uncertain waters.

Ecumenists who care about the next generation placed me in actual situations where the unity of the Church was experienced, struggled with and tested.

I learned that authentic ecumenism requires leaders of deep faith and commitment to the Gospel who approach each other with respect and humility, eagerly learning from other Christian traditions, receiving the spiritual gifts and insights of each person and tradition as a sign of the Church universal.

The need for patience
I learned that holy impatience is sometimes a gift of God, but cannot bring the churches fully together in Christ. The processess of theological consensus – building and ecumenical praxis – have to go hand in hand.

Joan Delaney

MM (Maryknoll Missioner), Director of Mission Research at the Maryknoll Sisters Center in New York, USA. *Roman Catholic.*

IN MY ecumenical journey, I have become more and more convinced of the importance of the personal dimension in the ecumenical movement. When all is said and done, when the structures have been devised and the issues debated, it is the attitudes of people that either move the cause of unity forward or throw up obstacles which make the structure unworkable and the issues unresolvable. For this reason I regard personal attitudes as foundational to the ecumenical cause.

My own ecumenical experience was developed in a pre-Vatican II missionary situation. This would not be regarded as an ideal climate for an ecumenical experience. However, I was thrust into an ecumenical situation as the result of the need for a group of Christian schools to deal with a colonial government. The government had no intention of dealing with Christian schools denomination by denomination, so we were obliged to form one educational organization. The need for a united front *vis à vis* the government provided the situation which made us realize that we had more in common than the academic curriculum, financial needs and sports days. Through our discussions we discovered how many of our values were the same and how many of our differences were not as significant as we had tended to make them. Personal friendships formed across denominational lines, and while participation in each other's worship services was still more of an exception than the rule, a greater appreciation and understanding of each other's religious beliefs and practices developed.

I tend to return to this early ecumenical experience in an effort to find the key to some of my more recent ecumenical history, which involves six years of full time work in an ecumenical organization. After years of ecumenical discussions involving doctrinal questions, institutional arrangements and common projects, I have concluded that we have a pressing need to return periodically to that personal level and to examine ourselves on what I call 'ecumenical sensitivity'. This modern ecumenical virtue involves two dimensions: empathy and understanding

The capacity to enter into another's feelings is not inborn; it is developed. While some people may be more disposed to it than others, empathy can and should be cultivated in the ecumenical movement. It involves an ability to enter into another person's spiritual journey in a supportive way. I once found myself moderating a Bible study group of very disparate people. Acting on what I now realize must have been an inspiration of the Holy Spirit, I suggested that we begin our series of eight daily meetings not with the usual name and place identifications, but with a description of each individual's spiritual journey. The members responded with great sincerity, and while it consumed two entire meeting periods, the sharing proved invaluable. When differences arose, the participants had been so impressed by the rendition of the person's spiritual journey that there was a genuine and often moving effort to understand the other's position. This proved true in differences concerning how to deal with violence in South Africa and Northern Ireland, how God acted in history, how people can be saved if they have not heard the name of Jesus, and what constitutes the social message of the Gospel. These are hardly issues marked by feelings of indifference; and positions on them are often strongly influenced by the teachings of one's denomination.

In some ecumenical situations, I have been astounded as well as pained at how little effort is made to appreciate liturgical practices, organizational styles, types of behaviour and even dress in another religious tradition. One shudders at a type of ecumenical uniformity which hardly bespeaks unity. A willingness to accept a practice as meaningful for another does not mean that one cannot question its origin, and certainly does not imply that the questioner is expected to embrace the practice. There is a need to develop a manner that implies a real interest in, and appreciation of, whatever has spiritual meaning for another.

Some of the real breakthroughs of understanding on a deep level occur when we have put aside our preconceived ideas of what is ecumenically correct and try to enter into another's religious experience. It appears that while this is a cardinal tenet of the dialogue between Christians with those of other religious traditions (for example, Hindus, Muslims, Buddhists),it does not seem to have penetrated the ecumenical world to the same degree. The view that in our attempt to understand the other we are changed and the other is also changed needs to be underscored as occurring also in ecumenical discussions among Christians.

One of the many positive results of ecumenical sensitivity is a deepening of our desire 'to understand' the other ... to know why certain beliefs and practices are meaningful for that person. This should lead us to find out in a consistent and coherent way more about the religious beliefs of the particular denomination.

Here we meet another weakness that empathy will help us avoid. As we compare the belief system of the other with our own denominational beliefs and practices, we shall concern ourselves with establishing a consistency of belief. We shall try to establish the consistency between denominational belief and individual behaviour. We shall become aware of how belief motivates action but more importantly we shall come to recognize the intensity of feeling with which some beliefs are held. It is through this awareness of consistency and intensity that we will be better able to uncover the true nature of our differences and similarities. This should help us to move further along the road leading to a unity of minds and hearts. It is this aspect of unity that should free us to imagine other creative ways of being a more united faith community which speaks to the world of our oneness in Christ.

PRAYER

May the Christ who called us to be one in mind and heart, give us ears to hear the spiritual journey of the other;
May the Christ who called us to be one, make us more sympathetic to the religious views of the other;
May the Christ who admonished us to use our talents, inspire us to greater creativity and tenacity in promoting unity among all Christians. Amen.

Sentences for discussion

The personal dimension
In my ecumenical journey, I have become more and more convinced of the importance of the personal dimension in the ecumenical movement. When all is said and done, when the structures have been devised and issues debated, it is the attitudes of people that either move the cause of unity forward or throw up obstacles which make the structure unworkable and the issues unresolvable.

Empathy
The capacity to enter into another's feelings is not inborn; it is developed.
Empathy ... involves an ability to enter into another person's spiritual journey in a supportive way.

Faces of diversity
We discovered how many of our values were the same and how many of our differences were not as significant as we tended to make them.

One shudders at a type of ecumenical uniformity which hardly bespeaks unity. A willingness to accept a practice as meaningful for another, does not mean that one cannot question its origin and certainly does not imply that the questioner is expected to embrace the practice.

Alan D. Falconer

Formerly Director of the Irish School of Ecumenics; Director of the Faith and Order Commission Secretariat, World Council of Churches. *Reformed.*

IN HER important study on aspects of conversion in the New Testament, Beverly Gaventa identifies three categories of personal change.[1] The first category is 'alternation'. This is a relatively limited form of change which develops naturally from an individual's previous behaviour. It is a natural progression, where the roots of later developments can be identified in earlier stages of the person's growth and development. The second 'type' of change she identified is 'conversion', which is a radical change in which past affiliations are rejected and replaced by a new commitment and identity. The catalyst of such change may be an event, person, group or other agent which triggers the dramatic change in the individual's perceptions and values. The third mode of change identified is 'transformation' which is an altered perception reinterpreting both the present and the past. A transformation is a radical change of perspective in which some newly gained cognition brings about a changed way of understanding. Unlike a conversion, a transformation does not require a rejection or negation of the past or of previously held values. Instead a transformation involves a new perception, a re-cognition, of the past. As with conversion, however, the catalyst of change is an event, person, group or other agent.[2] Transformation is a continuing process – a series of 'moments' or 'events' where the horizon is transfigured.

It is this category of 'transformation' which comes closest to encapsulating the decisive encounters, events and experiences in my own ecumenical pilgrimage. I was born into a church-going family, and it was evident that an equation was being made by my parents between being 'Scottish' and being 'Presbyterian'. Chance remarks or football team allegiances gave the impression of an incompatibility be-tween being Scottish and Roman Catholic and to a slightly lesser extent being Scottish and Episcopalian.[3] This family atmosphere was reinforced by the celebrations in my mid-teenage years of the Quater-centenary of the Scottish Reformation. This was evident throughout the country in special television programmes, newspaper articles, exhibi-tions and publications centred on the meeting of the General Assembly of the Kirk. Perhaps the fact that my parish minister was one of the foremost Scottish Reforma-tion historians led to my own heightened awareness of the specific contribution of this churchmanship to the life of the nation and of the wider world.

Towards the end of my school days I had imbibed this attitude that 'Scottish Presbyterianism is best' and 'Roman Catholicism is to be denigrated' sufficiently to make some anti-Roman Catholic remarks. On hearing these, one of my peers commented 'That's not a very Christian thing to say'. It was a simple remark – yet one which proved to have the quality of a 'kairos', a decisive moment, for me. Since there were no Roman Catholics in my school, street or immediate vicinity the course I found myself adopting was that of reading some basic works on Roman Catholic life and thought, and attending Mass at the local Roman Catholic Cathedral. Within the evangelical fellowship of which I was Prayer Secretary with the responsibility for designating topics for prayer, we began to pray for the Second Vatican Council – but not, as might have been the case, so that 'they' might 'see the truth'!

Later in theological college, this encounter with Roman Catholic thought was deepened for me through study of the Council under the guidance of Professor J. K. S. Reid. He had attended the Council as an 'observer' on behalf of the World Alliance of Reformed Churches. Such study led to a widening of my theological horizons. Of course, it was not uncritical of aspects of Roman Catholic thought, but such criticism was always within the framework of appreciation of the central affirmations of the theology and witness of that tradition. Such an encounter with Roman Catholic theology demonstrated also the interdependence of Roman Catholic and Presbyterian histories and emphases. It was impossible to understand Presbyterian or Reformed theology and polity without an appreciation of its rootedness in a wider and older European theological tradition.

The study of the Second Vatican Council showed me that the Roman Catholic Church is not monolithic in structure nor monosyllabic in theological expression. The wide range of views represented at the Council destroyed any possibility of remaining content with a stereotypical '-ism'. The lively engagement with the central issues facing Christians in the contemporary world emphasised the importance of collaborating with Roman Catholics on a wide variety of issues, and of listening to individuals so that they could articulate for themselves how they understood their life and work in the context of their faith commitment.

It was to be a decade later, when I joined the staff of the Irish School of Ecumenics in Dublin, before all this was even more vividly evident, because I then moved into a situation of living and working in a predominantly Roman Catholic environment. So the encounter with Roman Catholic thought and life, sparked off by the chance remark of a peer, led to a widening of the horizon of what it meant to be Christian. This did not lead to a rejection or negation of the past. Rather, there was a new perception, a re-cognition of the past. 'Transformation' occurred in my thinking.

A second important 'moment' or 'event' in my ecumenical pilgrimage took place when I was still a theological student. Awarded a small scholarship to explore a centre of theological renewal in Europe, I attended a course at the Ecumenical Institute at Bossey. The seminar was concerned with the Theology and Spirituality of the Orthodox churches. In dialogue with Orthodox scholars – Nikos Nissiotis, Olivier Clement, Boris Bobrinskoy – the riches of the traditions of the Eastern Churches' thought and life were presented. The theoretical part of the seminar was then reinforced by participation in the Holy Week celebrations with members of the parish and community of the Institut St Serge in Paris. The meeting with Christians of another tradition seriously engaged in wrestling with Christian thought and witness forced me to listen seriously to their tradition and to seek to understand that which seemed uncongenial.

Exposure to Nikos Nissiotis's lectures on icons then and in later years even led to an appreciation of icons and iconography.[4] The rich liturgical tradition, the profound theology of the Holy Spirit, the participation of one's whole being in praise to the Holy Trinity, shook me to the core, and led me to explore again the riches of ecclesiology, of the understanding of the Holy Spirit and of engagement in mission, in the light of the story of the development of the Alaskan Mission by Innocenti and others. The encounter was one of renewal, with all the pain and joy which that entails. The experience of worship at St Serge also made a powerful impact on me. The re-enactment of the drama of Holy Week began to lead to an appreciation of the aloneness and dereliction of the crucifixion. The demeanour of the worshippers whose Bridegroom was dead has left an indelible mark on my own spirituality and attitude to worship, as has their joy at the resurrection.

After the initial shock of the encounter with the Eastern churches, a changed way of understanding Christianity began to emerge in me – not negating the past but transforming it through a renewed appreciation of, and wrestling with, questions concerning the nature of the Church. A greater sense of awe and wonder at the manifold gifts and expressions of the Holy Spirit heightened an overall extending of my horizons in appreciating the faith. Transformation took place gradually but perceptibly.

As with my encounter with Roman Catholic life and thought, I found it very difficult to communicate to others within my own tradition the insights and gifts evident in Eastern life and thought. I was perceived as having 'betrayed' my tradition. A tension existed between the commitments to a specific ecclesial community, and commitment to the wider vision of the Christian faith than that shared by many of my contemporaries.[5] To try to overcome this, I took part in discussions on comparative aspects of Reformed and Orthodox traditions, and framed exploratory liturgies which incorporated elements of, and emphasised the basic movement, of the Divine Liturgy. At first I consciously included in discussions, sermons and articles appropriate quotations from writers of the Orthodox tradition, until such time as a greater fusion of the insights of Roman Catholic and Orthodox thought with that of my Reformed heritage should make them familiar – after all, John Calvin made extensive use of the writings of the Cappadocian Fathers[6] in his work. The encounters with Roman Catholic and Eastern Orthodox thought were fundamental for the process of transformation, and for my commitment to the search for Christian unity.

A third decisive 'moment' or 'event' in my ecumenical pilgrimage was my participation as a student in the Graduate School of Ecumenical Studies at the Ecumenical Institute at Bossey. In this residential setting I was privileged to study with pastors and lay people from every part of the world and from every conceivable tradition. Under the guidance of Hans-Ruedi Weber, Nikos Nissiotis and Michael Keeling, the Graduate School sought to explore deep issues of Christian commitment and action in relation to the question of revolutions throughout the world. All of us sought, out of shared Christian commitment, to engage in a common exploration, drawing on the resources of our cultures and confessional traditions.

This sharing with a Presbyterian pastor from a Frelimo-held area in Mozambique, a Baptist from North East Brazil, Czechoslovak, East German and Russian pastors and priests, and colleagues from Asia, North and South America, the Pacific, and other parts of Europe, has made it a different and difficult experience to read a newspaper ever since. Awareness of our interrelatedness and interdependence, and our common citizenship of our global village expanded my horizon of God's involvement in the total human enterprise. It led to a greater commitment to the search for the unity of the Church for the sake of humankind. A further transformation, then, induced a radical change of perspective – a change which again did not involve a rejection or negation of the past, but a re-cognition of it. These decisive moments have been reinforced by further encounters with Christians of other traditions and cultures over the years. I have been fortunate in receiving these gifts of other people, and in having the opportunity to share in a number of events – bilateral and multilateral dialogues, work for human rights protection and promotion, and world Christian assemblies – all of which have demonstrated the wonderful riches of the presence of God. As I try to reflect on my pilgrimage, I am conscious of the breaking-in of others and the Other, transforming and transfiguring my convictions, commitments and attempts to articulate the inexpressible. That is why I have described my ecumenical pilgrimage as a process involving transformations.

PRAYER

*Father in heaven! What is a man without You! What
is all he knows, vast accumulation though it be, but a
chipped fragment if he does not know You! What is
all his striving, could it even encompass a world, but
a half-finished work if he does not know You: You the
One, who art one thing and who art all! So may You
give to the intellect, wisdom to comprehend You; to
the heart, sincerity to receive this understanding; to
the will, purity that wills only You.*

Søren Kierkegaard. *Purity of Heart is to Will One Thing*

Sentences for discussion

Challenges
Towards the end of my schooldays I had imbibed this atti-

tude of 'Scottish Presbyterianism is best' and 'Roman Catholicism is to be denigrated' sufficiently to make some anti-Roman Catholic remarks. On hearing these, one of my peers commented, 'That's not a very Christian thing to say'. A simple remark – yet one which proved to have the quality of a 'kairos' – a decisive moment for me.

A major difficulty occurred in trying to communicate to others within my own tradition the insights and gifts evident in eastern life and thought. I was perceived as having 'betrayed' my tradition!

The encounter was one of renewal, with all the pain and joy which that entails.

Contextualization
It was impossible to understand Presbyterian or Reformed theology and polity without an appreciation of its rootedness in a wider European theological tradition.

NOTES

1. Beverly Gaventa, *From Darkness to Light: Aspects of Conversion in the New Testament* (Philadelphia, 1986).

2. Cf. Hans Küng's 'paradigm shift'.

3. It was not until one year ago that I came to realize that for my father this attitude to Roman Catholics derived from the Edinburgh gang fights of the 1930s between Protestants and Roman Catholics.

4. This was especially significant for the heir of a Reformation community to whom icons were anathema.

5. A helpful discussion of this tension is given in the recent report of the Groupe des Dombes, *For the Conversion of the Churches* (Geneva, WCC, 1993).

6. The fourth century bishop-theologians Basil the Great, Gregory Nazianzus and Gregory of Nyssa.

Kyriaki Karidoyanes Fitzgerald

Theologian, serving on the Faith and Order Commission of the World Council of Churches, representing the Ecumenical Patriarch of Constantinople. *Eastern Orthodox.*

QUITE FRANKLY, I found myself participating in ecumenical work because I was asked to. After all, I felt that I entered Orthodox theological seminary in order to grow in my relationship with God, serve God and his people, and if God wanted me to serve here or there, well, so be it. I would go. Sometimes, I would respond so eagerly that heaven and earth could not stop me. Pity those who had to deal with my enthusiasm!

Part of my wholehearted, eager and naïve (read: uncritical) response may be related to the fact that I chose to enter the seminary right out of high school. In other words, I actually came to Orthodox seminary wholeheatedly, eagerly, naively. I was also very young. Needless to say, and without my conscious knowing, the experience gained by responding to virtually every call to 'represent the Church' at ecumenical gatherings (even as a student), somehow gave me another context to apply the valuable lessons I had been learning at seminary. I was too grateful for every invitation to consider that my presence was required as the token Orthodox female. Paradoxically, and despite this subtle, underlying negative context, theological dialogue has evolved into an important part of my life's work.

Yet in virtually all of these opportunities for theological dialogue, I never could escape the fact that I was an Orthodox Christian woman. I frequently found myself feeling as if I were a kind of 'ecumenical oddity'. My particular seminary experience, training and theology would usually be different from that of my American female colleagues. There seemed, sadly enough, to be no heart-felt urgency to increase the ration of Orthodox female theologians serving on the delegations to these ecumenical meetings.

Nevertheless, as I became more familiar with the theological and ecumenical terrain, I soon learned that at an 'official' level I was doing what I often do on an 'everyday' level. And this, while simultaneously appreciating diversity, is to seek for the underlying coherence and integrity presented to me on an inter-personal level. In so doing, I have begun to learn a number of important lessons, which pertain to life and the greater Church. Three of the most important lessons concern: the 'good news; the 'bad news'; and the 'ability to be grateful'. I will briefly share them now.

The good news
The first lesson has to go with the 'good news', the Gospel. I have learned from the very start of ecumenical work that we, the various divided Christian communities, are somehow still connected to the underlying 'good news', the Gospel of our risen Lord, Jesus Christ. This 'good news' essentially conveys two messages.

The first message is concerned with relationship. God has emptied himself (*kenosis*) through the process of becoming human, living with us, dying for us (because of us) and returning to us, as our risen Lord and Friend. Our Lord's life-giving and mysterious and unique sacrifice heals and even re-creates the previously broken relationship between the Triune God and humanity. Despite the unfathomable pain involved in this sacrifice, Jesus did this for us *cheerfully*, I believe. He is still cheerful, today, at the thought of each of us, despite our personal falling short of everything good. There is no other theology about which I am aware, which proclaims this kind of relationship between a loving Triune God and human persons.

The bad news
As time went on, I gained more exposure to people from my own and other faith communities. I also learned more about the 'bad news'. The bad news is essentially anything which is set up against the good news. The bad news seeks dominion over the good news. The bad news diverts our

attention away from the loving God of the 'good news'. This is a kind of negative audacious power, a power which would be 'god'.

Simply by being human we are daily assailed by the bad news. The bad news takes many forms. It assails us from without, in many ways, not the least of which include: human complacency, negativity, abuse, oppression of the poor and weak, sexism and abandonment on many, many levels. The loving God is apparently absent in the midst of this bad news.

The bad news also assails us from within. It assails us through what we in Eastern Christianity often refer to as 'hardness of heart'. Hardness of heart locks the presence of the living God out of the core of who we are. We cannot change and grow if our hearts are hard. It is through this kind of hardness that we actually prevent the Holy Spirit of God from growing in relationship with us. It is how people remain static and ultimately die to their own true identity as unique sons and daughters of the living God. This is because the bad news bears no fruit; it gives no life.

Our present state of divided Christianity somehow serves the bad news, I believe. There are numerous persons in the ecumenical world who glibly take our fragmented situation for granted on a spiritual level. Taking our divisions for granted reflects our personal deafness to the scandal of Christian alienation. This assumption leads to a dead end. This is because the had news bears no fruit. It gives no life.

The ability to be grateful

The Psalmist proclaims: 'The sacrifice acceptable to God is a broken spirit; a broken and contrite heart, O God, you will not despise' (Psalm 50/1. 17). It is only those whose hearts have been broken who can experience the depths of God's loving-tenderness. This is a bold statement to make. Some of us may cynically ask, 'Only those ... am I not saved?' Some of us theologians may even dare to ask, 'Am I not one of the elect?' This cynical and narcissistic stance makes us wonder what remains frozen in the psyche. Sometimes we are frozen and do not know it. At other times, we may even not want to know. And at still other times, we are frozen, and we do know, and wish we did not. It takes tremendous courage and discipline to confront our frozen inner places which keep out the living God. It is hard work to be aware of our own self-centered propensities which keep us from authentic relationships and the abundant life. As we honestly take stock and suffer with the confusion and resulting darkness, we slowly find ourselves opening to the inrushing presence of God filling the darkness with his light and presence ... if only for a little bit ...

It is here, where, I believe, the Christian 'stance' in life, ecumenical and otherwise, comes. It is a stance which gratefully stands antithetically to the bad news of our divisions. It is a stance which gratefully sings praises to the loving God even in the midst of isolation and darkness. It is a stance which gratefully says in the Spirit, 'Yes, come Lord Jesus!' even in the very depths of our failures. It is the stance which I believe Christians must strive to keep today. It is a stance which can only be rooted in 'Christ Jesus, our hope' (I Timothy 1.1).

PRAYER

O thrice-blessed Lord, it is you who have called us
and all creatures back to yourself; and you, Lord
Jesus, who prayed that we all be one. Look now on
us, your sinful and broken people, and have mercy on
us; as our present state betrays your desire. Let your
ever-present loving tenderness end our pride, purify
our hearts, heal our wounds, renew our strength and
restore our vision; so that, serving you, our witness
will move truly give you praise, glory and honour,
Father, Son and Holy Spirit, unto the ages of ages.
Amen.

Sentences for discussion

Division is bad news
Our present state of divided Christianity somehow serves the bad news, I believe. There are numerous persons in the ecumenical world who glibly take our fragmented situation for granted on a spiritual level. Taking our divisions for granted reflects our personal deafness to the scandal of Christian alienation.

The risk and the reward
As we honestly take stock and suffer with the confusion and resulting darkness, we slowly find ourselves opening to the inrushing presence of God filling the darkness with his light and presence ... if only for a little bit ...

Dean Freiday

Member and past clerk of the Christian and Interfaith Relations Committee of Friends General Conference, Philadelphia, USA. *Religious Society of Friends.*

IN THE thirty-five years that I have been ecumenically involved, I have come to the conclusion that what you can learn from those you meet far outweighs any tangible or measurable contribution that you are likely to make. This is particularly true for me as a representative of a tiny group which numbers a little over 300,000 Quakers of all varieties worldwide. Yet we should never lose sight of the fact that the lives and witness of twelve Apostles changed the world – turned it 'upside down' (Acts 17.6). And even in our century individuals with names like Tutu, Teresa, or King have reached the hearts of those who have never seen nor heard them, as well as giving hope to those living lives of desperation and degradation.

A flourishing local council of fifty-two member churches succumbed quickly when a new group of pastors was just not interested. Christ's call to continue building community and understanding across both denominational and racial boundaries, which had flourished almost miraculously for a few years, was no longer heard. The council died some twenty-five years ago and has never been revived. But while this Red Bank, New Jersey, council did function, it owed a great deal to a young housewife who served endless hours as an unsalaried volunteer secretary. Gretchen Williams, as her name was, was particularly skillful at finding out when one of the council's projects was on dead center and just who it was who had dropped the ball. Then she would tactfully goad the responsible person into action. All this was done behind the scenes and with almost no public knowledge of what had happened. As far as we know, Christ never had a secretary, although the Apostle Paul made clear his indebtedness to a whole cadre of them.

The nearest thing to a 'living apostle' (that is, one who somehow reminds you of the original first-century model) whom I have known was Bishop Mar Athanasius, the Missionary Bishop of the Mar Thoma Church. At first glance, he was a strange sight to a Quaker, with his small curled black cap with white crosses on it. He alternated between baby blue and baby pink ankle-length robes. When asked about the liturgical significance of the alternation, he confided that there was none. Cleanliness was the governing factor. One could be washed and dried while the other was worn.

A group of us at the Fourth World Conference on Faith and Order at Montreal (1963), where we met him, were very pleased when he agreed to our request for him to sit at the head of our table for meals, because dignity and humility combined in him to make for both impeccable behaviour and easy approachability. In his frequent travels he held widely scattered little pockets of Mar Thoma Christians together by accepting their hospitality for christenings, weddings and other family-community events.

Others I have met ecumenically have often exemplified what it means to be a Christian in quite unspectacular yet inescapable ways. You soon learn that none of us, denominationally speaking, has a monopoly on the apostolate. Nor do apostles come in easily recognizable types or ranks. The biggest mistake you can make is to stereotype them on the basis of position. It is as bad to assume on the one hand that because they have successfully achieved 'high office' they are bound to be humdingers; as it is to assume that just because of their office they are not 'good Christians'.

Another person at Montreal (I could easily name half a dozen) who made a lasting impression on me was an Observer for the North American Baptist General Conference (popularly known as German Baptists, and which although only about 50,000 in United States membership produced Walter Rauschenbusch of Social Gospel fame). This observer virtually exuded Christian spirituality of a special type. It was a blessing just to talk with him. His life had been so shaped by his Christian faith that it un-obtrusively reached you, made you feel ministered to and eager for more. But something more than an ascetically 'formed' (in the broadest sense) spirituality is found in genuine apostles.

Two New Testament phrases give a clue. In our mission to the world, we should be 'wise as serpents, harmless as doves' (Matthew 10.16). In dealing with Christians, I always assume that it is not necessary to be as wary as that. I try to approach them as Israelites 'in whom is no guile' (John 1.47). I do not think I am a naïve person, but the high expectations I have placed on those I meet ecumenically have only really been abused twice, once locally and once internationally. That does not mean that I have not been stereotyped frequently, sometimes by inference, sometimes overtly, as representing a 'peculiar little sect'. What it does say is that any apostle worth his salt is trustworthy not manipulative, and that generalizing either trait as though it were typical of a given denomination is as wrong as making slurs on the basis of abuses by some members of a given group.

A uniform is another non-indication of an apostle. Uniforms are tremendously helpful in identifying a potential source of help for those who need it, whether they be Franciscan, Salvation Army, Methodist Deaconness, or some other. However, the uniforms are far from providing final clues as to what an apostle does or does not look like. God created us all as individuals, not clones. He alone knows our full potential. He alone can give us the grace to be 'imitators' of his Son. He alone can pick us up and brush us off when we stumble, 'backslide', or fall; though he may have human helpers. But the choice to be apostles – living exemplars of the Christian faith – is ours. To be an apostle is neither as easy nor as glamorous as it might at first appear. A cross often precedes our 'resurrection' too.

The joy of knowing in our hearts that on some points at least we have been truly apostles has to be experienced rather than described. But what elation, what joy, to know that we have been faithful servants of our Risen Lord.

PRAYER

May the Spirit of Christ ever attend our efforts on his behalf. May we always be open to see Christ in those who are in need. May we also, whatever their faith may be, recognize those who are channels of his grace in meeting those needs.

This we ask in the name of the Father and of the Son and of the Holy Spirit.

Sentences for discussion

The ecumenical apostolate
Individuals with names like Tutu, Teresa or King have reached the hearts of those who have never seen nor heard them, as well as giving hope to those living lives of desperation and degradation.

What you can learn from those you meet far outweighs any tangible or measurable contribution that you are likely to make.

Others I have met ecumenically have often exemplified what it means to be a Christian in quite unspectacular yet inescapable ways.

You soon learn that none of us, denominationally speaking, has a monopoly on the apostolate.

Any apostle worth his salt is trustworthy not manipulative.

Günther Gassmann

Formerly Director of the Commission on Faith and Order of the World Council of Churches (1987-94). *Lutheran.*

WE WERE a Christian youth group of high school pupils in a small town in Thuringia, at that time in the German Democratic Republic. The communist régime began to dominate all areas of life; liberties like the open expression of one's opinion or the travel to western countries were abolished. Life became restricted and the awareness of being caught up in a large prison became part of our daily existence. The Christian youth group was for us one of the few open spaces where we could feel free and move among like-minded people.

In this group, in the years 1946–1950, our pastor told us about the ecumenical movement and the early activities of the World Council of Churches. Some publications, leaflets and journals reached us, and for me a window was opened in our prison. I began to grasp something of a wider, in fact world-wide Christian family, which surrounded us and to which we belonged despite being kept in this pseudo-socialist cage. This was a great consolation and encouragement: we felt that we were not alone, we were not finally cut off from the rest of the world, we were part of a community which transcends all political and other barriers.

At that time one could still cross the border from East to West Germany – sitting in the night behind bushes and waiting until the frontier guards had passed by. I studied theology at the University of Heidelberg in West Germany and immediately began to attend seminars on ecumenical theology. My earlier liberating experience of realizing that we were part of a larger Christian community was now deepened and broadened by knowledge, reflection and a clearer and now realistic sense of the agreements and differences and even barriers within the world-wide Christian community. I continued to give special attention to doing theology in an ecumenical perspective. I became assistant to my teacher, Professor Edmund Schlink, who was among the leading ecumenists between 1950 and 1980, and I experienced ecumenism during a year in an Anglican theological college in Oxford in England, and as director of the Ecumenical Student House in Heidelberg.

Thus, the foundations for an 'ecumenical life' had been laid during my time in school and university. These foundations were, in a way, contextual and existential and not purely theoretical. From then on my biography was marked by a kind of ecumenical logic: work in the Institute for Ecumenical Research in Strasbourg, France, involvement in several bilateral dialogues while head of the central office of the Lutheran churches in West Germany, ecumenical officer of the Lutheran World Federation in Geneva and, since 1984, Director of the Secretariat of the Commission on Faith and Order within the World Council of Churches in Geneva.[1]

I have learned and, I hope, kept alive, two lessons from my own ecumenical journey. The first is that ecumenism begins with experience. It is through encounters and exposure to specific situations that interest and awareness are awakened. It remains, therefore, an important task for congregations, groups and theological seminaries to provide for such occasions where these initial experiences that create an 'appetite for more' can take place.

And a second lesson, rooted in my initiation experience into ecumenism during my school days, has marked and shaped my ecumenical conviction and teaching: ecumenical commitment and involvement opens up our limited or narrow ecclesial and national horizons. The experience of an already existing real communion between the Christian churches and the theological and practical work for deepening this communion provides us with a fascinating vision as well as concrete experience of 'the whole Christian Church on earth' (Martin Luther). That is most comforting and enriching, and the main and joyful impetus for my own Christian and ecumenical existence.

This already existing real communion and the need to further deepen it was also at the centre of the Fifth World Conference on Faith and Order held at Santiago de Compostela in Spain in August 1993. There we prayed:

O God,
All life and grace are coming from you.
Open our hearts and minds
To the insights and experiences of our
Brothers and Sisters in other Christian traditions
So that we become enriched and renewed
By sharing of your gifts among us
Being already now in communion with all
Who believe in you,
Perfect union of Father, Son and Holy Spirit
We ask this in Christ's name. Amen.

Sentences for discussion

Personal experience
Ecumenism begins with experience. It is through encounters and exposure to specific situations that interest and awareness are awakened.

Belonging
This was a great consolation and encouragement: we are not alone, we are not finally cut off from the rest of the world.

NOTES
1. Retiring at the time of publication.

Paulos Mar Gregorios

Metropolitan of Delhi, President Inter-Religious Federation for World Peace, New York,USA. Former President, World Council of Churches. *Oriental Orthodox.*

UNTIL 1959, I was rather hostile to the World Council of Churches, which had been formally founded in Amsterdam, a very Calvinist city, only in 1948. My negative attitude was despite the fact that I had acquired considerable ecumenical experience through student organisations like the Geneva-based World Student Christian Federation and the Student Christian Movement of India, of which I was Honorary Secretary from 1954 to 1956. My disapproval came from the fact that I regarded the WCC as too Western and too Protestant to be genuinely ecumenical. I was in America as a theological student at Princeton at the time of the Second Assembly in Evanston, in 1954, but I made no attempt to attend despite the fact that my church had nominated me as an alternative delegate. So my interest in the WCC was scant, perhaps due to unjustified prejudices.

In the summer of 1959, after resigning my job as Private Secretary and Advisor to Emperor Haile Selassie of Ethiopia, I spent two weeks at the Ecumenical Institute in Bossey near Geneva. This gave me a new perspective. I saw that my Christian faith was invigorated and stimulated by the exchange of views with Christians of other cultures, nations and confessions.

I was on my way to Yale for a Doctoral program in Theology and Philosophy. My teachers at the Divinity School were all, of course, Protestants, some of them, like Professor Robert Calhoun and Professor Richard Niebuhr, very distinguished indeed. I respected not only their immense erudition and integrity but also their willingness to admit that they knew practically nothing about the tremendous wealth of Eastern Christian thought and spirituality.

In reacting further from Protestant thought – earlier, at

Princeton, I had reacted rather strongly against the ilk of Barth and Brunner – I was helped by the fact that the Theology Department of Yale Divinity School had graciously granted that I need not listen to any more Protestant theology lectures but could pursue my own research into such Orthodox literature as was available at Yale Divinity School Library. The only requirement was that I should read a one-hour paper on Orthodox Theology every week to Professor Claude Welch, the head of the Department of Theology. Whether Claude Welch benefited from my papers or not (I rather think he did), those were practically my first (self-taught) lessons in formal Orthodox theology.

Since I found Yale Divinity School unable to meet my requirements in instruction and guidance in the field of the apostolic heritage of the Christian Church, I moved, with the generous help of Yale Divinity School Dean Liston Pope, to Oxford as a D.Phil student. There again I found little understanding of my Orthodox heritage. It was while at Oxford (1960) that I was invited to Geneva by Dr Visser't Hooft, the General Secretary of the WCC, who formally requested me to take up a staff position in the World Council of Churches. I told him my view, that the WCC was too Trans-Atlantic and too Protestant for my taste. He readily agreed and rather cleverly responded that that was the precise reason why he wanted me on the staff – to correct that imbalance. I suggested that one person on the staff could not correct such an imbalance. I did not accept the offer and went back to Oxford for my doctoral studies.

Then came the Third Assembly (1961) of the WCC in New Delhi. That was what pushed me into the mainstream of the ecumenical movement. I was impressed by the fact that Protestants were just as much receptive as the Orthodox to all my Bible studies (perhaps even more). Here I became convinced of the ecumenical nature of the Christian Scriptures, and Bible study became an integral part of my ecumenical ministry afterwards.

The important thing that people remember about the New Delhi Assembly was the large scale 'coming in' of the

Orthodox churches from behind 'The Iron Curtain' into the membership and fellowship of the WCC. In November 1961, after the Assembly was over, all the Orthodox delegates present went south (a good 3000 kilometres) to Kerala, to visit my church. They persuaded the *Catholicos* of my church that I should take up, on their behalf, the position of Associate General Secretary of the WCC and Director of its Division of Ecumenical Action, with headquarters in Geneva. I was rather reluctant to leave my studies at Oxford, but I had to respond positively to the united Orthodox demand that I go, on condition that I would serve no more than five years. I had thus joined the 'Ecumenical Establishment' by early 1962. Though I left the staff in 1967 as I had said I would (despite powerful persuasion to stay on in Geneva), I was hooked to the movement.

During the five years I stayed on the staff, my ecumenical experience, as well as my knowledge of the world, was immensely enriched. Though most of my services were to the Protestant churches of the world, I was able also significantly to serve the Orthodox churches and in addition to become more closely acquainted with the inner workings of the great Roman Catholic Church. I was privileged to be an Observer at the Second Vatican Council and to serve for twelve years as a member of the high-powered Joint Working Group between the WCC and the Roman Catholic Church. Even after leaving the WCC staff, I continued to be deeply involved in the whole ecumenical movement. I served on the Central and Executive Committees of the WCC, the Commission on Faith and Order, the Committee on Church and Society, the Dialogue Working Group, the Churches' Commission on Participation in Development, the Program to Combat Racism and many other bodies.

It was in 1968 that I became aware of what appeared to me an intense Protestant fear of losing control of the WCC. Many people at the Fourth Assembly of the WCC (Uppsala, 1968) wanted me to give leadership to the WCC and to the ecumenical movement as Chairman of the Central Committee. Again at the Vancouver Assembly in 1985, there was a concerted move on the part of many delegates to elect me as Moderator of the Central Committee. They, many of them Protestants, believed that I could rescue the WCC from its heavy Protestant orientation. This was prevented by nominating me as a President, a largely decorative post. When an Orthodox person with a modicum of competence appears on the horizon of the World Council of Churches, many Protestants seem to be scared that leadership may slip out of their hands. Neither do many Protestants seem to be willing to let the Roman Catholic Church with its huge political, economic and intellectual power exercise her rightful role in the leadership of the ecumenical movement. It seems to me that there has been a problem here throughout the half-century of the history of the WCC.

I have seen the dynamism of the ecumenical movement shift from the center to the periphery. At the same time, the movement gains momentum at the local level, where ecumenical bodies have become highly active and creative. Their pioneering and creativity offer hope for the future of the ecumenical movement. But they will not be very productive unless they maintain a global perspective and an attitude of openness in both culture and in spirituality. The growing pressures for such openness should be welcomed and responded to. The local councils should both see the Christian Church as existing for all of humanity on the one hand, and at the same time, be vigilant not to blur the distinctions that really matter.

It seems that a genuine ecumenical movement, profoundly spiritual, vigorous and comprehensive, rooted in prayer and true faith, and with a concern for the whole of humanity, for all life and for the interconnected web of the created order, which includes all the traditions, has a great and bright future. There are some hopeful signs on the horizon. The West is slowly breaking out into genuine cultural openness; there is more effective interreligious dialogue. There is not as yet sufficient willingness to accept responsibility for acknowledging mistakes. The practical expression of repentance will go a long way to opening up new vistas and avenues for the ecumenical movement as such.

PRAYER

Lord, all good things come from Thee. At mid-century you showed us a great vision. By our own failure to rise to the majestic scope of your call, our vision has gone dim. Rekindle in us Your love for all humanity and for all creation, so that the vision may glow again and beckon us beyond our own narrow horizons. May we press on beyond our cultural and religious parochialism to approach that reality of an integrated, united created order. Grant us the vision, the wisdom and the power to move humbly and resolutely to that Unity which You will.   Amen.

Sentences for discussion

Scripture
I was impressed by the fact that Protestants were just as much (perhaps even more) receptive as the Eastern Orthodox to all my Bible studies. Here I became convinced of the ecumenical nature of the Christian Scriptures, and Bible study became an integral part of my ecumenical ministry afterwards.

A stimulus to faith
My Christian faith was invigorated and stimulated by exchange of views with Christians of other cultures, nations and confessions.

81

Stanley Samuel Harakas

Archbishop Iakovos Professor of Orthodox Theology, Holy Cross
Greek Orthodox School of Theology, Brookline, Massachusetts,
USA. *Eastern Orthodox.*

THE NORTHWEST Airlines flight from Boston to Hong Kong
was not crowded, and I had plenty of space to stretch out
when I slept during the long journey. With so few passengers to attend to, the stewardesses gave the passengers
special attention. I thought that this augured well for my
trip to China as part of a special visitation team from the
'Justice, Peace and the Integrity of Creation' Unit of the
World Council of Churches to investigate the status of the
Christian churches in Guondong Province (formerly known
as Canton). The Director of the Unit, Raymond Fong, the
head of our small group of five, was returning home for the
first time in many years. Definitely this was to be a special
ecumenical event for all concerned, including the Chinese
Christians whom we would be visiting.

Our assignment was to visit on site a number of Christian
communities, organisations and activities, so as to assess
the condition of the Christian Church in China and to make
some recommendation about the proposed membership of
the Chinese churches in the World Council of Churches.
The members of the visitation team gathered in Hong Kong
as the staging point for our departure into Guondong
Province. My flight plans brought me to that teeming city
two days early, on January 4, 1989. I found my room waiting for me at the YMCA[1] hotel, and I had a chance to
explore some areas of this exotic city as the other members
of the team arrived.

First Experiences
Early on January 7, we boarded a train and left the bright,
colourful and flashing lights of Hong Kong for the contrasting drabness of Communist China.

Yet, in spite of those appearances, our experience in China was filled with a multitude of beautiful encounters which I can only briefly mention in anticipation of sharing more fully just one in the Protestant church of Guondong city.

It was with a sense of tension and not a little anxiety that we passed through the border check presided over by austere soldiers. Upon our arrival in the first Chinese city across the border, we were treated to a multi-course Chinese luncheon fit for royalty. When we arrived in Guondong and settled in our hotel, we began a series of visits. What a rich and memorable experience! Early in our itinerary were the offices of the Guondong Council of (Protestant) Churches, where we conversed with Christian confessors and martyrs who suffered imprisonment and the loss of position and property because of their Christian faith. We visited a Seminary, which not only conducted regular classes but also sponsored a full program of lay-education. The student dorms consisted of a single long hall with bunk beds on either side — hardly acceptable to our American seminarians. Then there was the surprise in the discovery of a replica of Paris's Notre Dame Cathedral in the midst of this Chinese metropolis. The Roman Catholic compound was showing signs of repair and rejuvenation following the excesses and persecutions of the Red Guards. We saw a new community of nuns in the process of formation.

At our session with the Chinese Roman Catholic Priest, the President of the Guondong Council of (Protestant) Churches was also present. We learned that they had been residents of the same city for decades and had never met each other. When both were forcibly removed from their positions by the Communists and the churches closed, both clergymen were forced to work as laborers in the same factory. It was there that they came to know of each other's Christian faith. They began to share their faith and to pray together, recollecting and discussing favorite passages of Scripture. Ecumenism began in persecution. They greeted each other in Christian love and spoke of their friendship in warm and endearing terms.

Guondong Chinese Christian Church

On Sunday morning our group followed a guide into a maze of buildings off a main bicycle-crowded street. Walking up and down sets of stairs and twisting hallways we finally arrived at the church. It was a typical nineteenth century building with a few stained glass windows. It could have been the reclaimed building in which I served in my first parish as a priest in Lancaster, Pennsylvania, before it was remodelled for Greek Orthodox use. A pulpit and a lectern were on the platform, with the communion table in a decidedly secondary place. To the left was a section for the choir. As the service started, a small number of choir members processed down the center aisle, while a larger number of choir members was already located in the choir area.

The service was a typical main-line Protestant worship service of the 1950s, with a call to worship, the singing of hymns by the congregation and choir anthem and the reading of Scripture. There being no ordained minister for the congregation, a woman of about seventy five years of age preached the sermon. My instincts told me that the sermon, which was an evangelical call to repentance and conversion, had been preached many times.

The congregation was well-dressed and quite mixed in age. There were elderly singles and spouses, young couples with children, a few young adults of both sexes; and all participated in the singing with vigor.

Following the service, we met with parish leaders and asked numerous questions. One of our group asked, 'Why do people come to a Christian church in this country?' The first answer surprised us: 'Because people like to sing, and the church is the only place where they can sing in public'. This led to attention to the choir and someone inquired, 'Why did only some of the choir process, while others were already in place?' The answer astonished us and led to an even more striking response regarding the appeal of the Church in Chinese Communist society. 'Well, you see, it is difficult for them to process because they are all blind!' 'The church,' one of our hosts explained, is the only place where disabled people are accepted and welcomed.' This expression of Christian compassion spoke volumes for the Christian way of life, we agreed.

We spent a beautiful day in another city where the Christians were permitted to establish an educational center for children suffering from a disease that required special processing of the waste produced by the children during their period of therapy. The Communist government permitted the establishment of this social service, since no one, not even the civil authorities, was interested in these unfortunate children. The Christians built large underground treatment tanks to take care of the physical problem, but also provided a full curriculum of education for about a hundred young children. I remember how they sang beautiful Chinese children's songs for us. We, in turn, sang songs for them. It was an exhilarating experience to see that the Christian way of life was indeed and markedly different from the materialistic culture of Communist China. The words of the Bible came to me with a new impact: 'But when Jesus perceived the thought of their hearts, he took a child and put him by his side, and said to them, 'Whoever receives this child in my name receives me, and whoever receives me receives him who sent me; for he who is least among you all is the one who is great' (Luke 9.47-48).

Reminiscences

Because of other commitments, I had to leave the WCC group early, to return home. Travelling alone on a Chinese train, I arrived late at night on January 11 in Hong Kong. I viewed the abruptly appearing bright Capitalist lights of Hong Kong, differently now. Amid the drabness of the Chinese environments I had found lights of a different sort — the spiritual lights that illumine the world in its spiritual darkness.

In the beginning was the Word, and the Word was with God, and the Word was God. He was in the beginning with God; all things were made through him, and without him was not anything made that was made. In him was life, and the life was the light of men. The light shines in the darkness, and the darkness has not overcome it' (John 1.1-5 Revised Standard Version)

I left Hong Kong on January 13, 1989, my fifty-seventh birthday. Only a few days later, the events of Tienemen Square began to unfold and the darkness became even darker in that vast land. But the light was still there. I was present at the Plenary of the World Council of Churches in Canberra, Australia, only a few years later, when the Chinese Church was received into membership. 'The light shines in the darkness, and the darkness has not overcome it.'

PRAYER

For the peace of the whole world, for the well-being of the Holy Churches of God and for the union of all, let us pray to the Lord. Lord have mercy.

From the Liturgy of St John Chrysostom

Sentences for discussion

No barriers

'The Church,' one of our hosts, explained, is the only place where disabled people are accepted and welcomed.' This expression of Christian compassion spoke volumes for the Christian way of life, we agreed.

Ecumenical friendship

When both were forcibly removed from their positions by the Communists and the churches closed, both clergymen were forced to work as laborers in the same factory. It was there that they came to know of each others' Christian faith. They began to share their faith and to pray together, recollecting and discussing favorite passages of Scripture. Ecumenism began in persecution.

Light in darkness

The events of Tienemen Square began to unfold and the darkness became even darker in that vast land. But the light was still there. I was present at the Plenary of the World Council of Churches in Canberra, Australia, only a few years later, when the Chinese Church was received into membership. 'The light shines in the darkness, and the darkness has not overcome it.'

NOTES

1. Young Men's Christian Association.

Christopher Hill

Canon Precentor of St Paul's Cathedral, London, England.
Formerly Secretary for Ecumenical Affairs to the Archbishop of
Canterbury. *Anglican.*

THE LATE Anglican bishop and philosopher, Ian Ramsey,
spoke of 'encounter experiences'. These were both ordinary
human experiences, and also moments of grace in which
there was something of conversion. The classical Biblical
story must be the dream of Jacob's Ladder – 'How awesome
is this place, this is nothing other than the House of God
and the gate of Heaven'.[1]

My ecumenical commitments have evolved over many
years, partly as an ecumenical bureaucrat serving three successive Archbishops of Canterbury, partly working in St
Paul's Cathedral where inevitably one is drawn to 'all sorts
and conditions' of people and where ecumenical ministry
must be second nature, but also from certain even more
basic human experiences in my earlier life. I will begin
there.

As a young boy in the West Midlands I got to know a
close friend of my mother's, a Roman Catholic lady who
sadly suffered from a disastrous marriage. Her husband left
her but she, within her Catholic piety, maintained the marriage and refused to consent to a divorce. (This was possible
in English Law in my boyhood.) She was responsible for
my earliest theological reading after a Sunday School prize
of Charles Kingsley's *The Water Babies* (which itself imbued
me with a primordial sense of Christian Socialism), My
mother's friend passed on to me C. S. Lewis's *The Screwtape
Letters*. One day I was walking in the nearby town of
Stourbridge, in Worcestershire, and I stepped into her
church – a Roman Catholic church dedicated to Our Lady
and St Thomas. I remember the feeling of nervous anxiety
as I stepped over the threshold, a feeling of being almost
traitorous to my own church. Roman Catholics of my

generation will have experienced the same thing entering an Anglican church or cathedral. But I was immediately able to pray there because it was 'her' church. I learned something about the unity of our Christian commitment. Some years later I went as a theological student on a pilgrimage to Taizé. I was a strictly disciplined High Anglican ordinand and I was conscious of the fact that I would not (then) have believed it right to receive communion from the Roman Catholic Church. At Taizé there was a daily Protestant Eucharist and a daily Roman Catholic Mass (celebrated by the Franciscans). Though I went to the Eucharist daily (alternating between the Protestant and Catholic celebrations), I did not feel able to receive communion. That experience was quite difficult for me, and it inspired me to take much more seriously the absolute necessity for the quest of Christian unity.

At my ordination to the diaconate, I was delighted to learn that my great uncle would attend. But he was a Methodist and, of course, I wanted him to receive communion at the ordination service. By this stage (1969) the Canon Law of the Church of England had been altered to allow such an ecumenical circumstance, and it gave me great delight that he could receive communion with me.

In my first parish, though, there was more than one Methodist Chapel, the vigorous Methodism of the Black Country (in the industrial Midlands of England) had by then degenerated into a number of feuding family chapels. Not much could be done ecumenically. The parish did have some contact with a neighbouring Roman Catholic church, but strictly speaking this was outside our parish boundary. The only lively Christian congregation other than the Anglican parish church and its mission churches happened to be an independent evangelical (and charismatic) tabernacle, some few hundred yards away from the mission church on the housing estate I served. It took some time to find common ground with the minister of this decidedly independent congregation. But we were able to come together during Christian Aid Week. Before that time there had been no systematic collections for Christian Aid throughout the parish. With the combined forces of a large evangelical community and an active Anglican parish we were able to raise more that £4,000 whereas the previous year the figure had been less than £100.

In my second parish there was both a vigorous Methodist church and a small but lively Roman Catholic church. Here a deep friendship with the Methodist minister and the Roman Catholic parish priest ensured a sincere commitment to unity on the part of the church communities. I well remember going to see the Roman Catholic parish priest to tell him that I would be moving to Lambeth Palace to work in the Ecumenical Office of the Archbishop and that one of my tasks would be that of the Anglican co-secretaryship of the Anglican-Roman Catholic International Commission. I was due to go to a meeting of the Commission near Rome that summer. The old parish priest smiled. He was fairly conservative in his tastes and convictions. But he trusted his Christian friendships. He said: 'I've never actually been to Rome, but when you go to St Peter's, light a candle for me and I will continue to pray for you'.

On moving to the 'foreign affairs' office at Lambeth Palace I became involved, of course, in a number of ecumenical committees and with a whole network of ecumenical correspondents. But it was always the human encounters which mattered most. I remember my amazement on discovering there were living Nestorians[2] in Ealing. (The so-called Assyrian Church assisted by the Archbishop of Canterbury's Assyrian mission in the nineteenth century.)

Friendships on the ARCIC Commission were and remain very important indeed. I recall the late Bishop Christopher Butler with the deepest veneration and affection. (He was a former Abbott of Downside and Auxiliary Bishop in Westminster.) When our first child died a still-born at eight months in the womb, many friends telephoned or wrote. But my wife and I still cherish the letter from Christopher Butler. Here was an old celibate Roman Catholic bishop and monk who also knew of the deepest human experiences and tragedies – as, of course, do all priests who take their ministry seriously.

During my fifteen years in the service of Archbishops of Canterbury at Lambeth there were many memorable ecumenical encounters. Amongst the most moving was the visit of the Pope to Canterbury Cathedral. The Pope (John Paul II), the Archbishop of Canterbury (Robert Runcie) and the Moderator of the Free Church Federal Council (Dr Kenneth Greet) together led the renewal of baptismal vows to a vast congregation in and outside the Cathedral and to millions more watching on television at the very site of the baptism of Southern England in Augustine's cathedral at Canterbury.

In quite a different setting, the visit of Archbishop Robert Runcie to the German Democratic Republic still comes vividly to mind. Many young Dresdeners came to receive communion from the Archbishop of Canterbury's hands on that Remembrance Day Sunday morning. They wore the badges of the churches' (unofficial) peace movement. At that time, the wearing of such a badge could have initiated immediate arrest by the police. In conversation with a sixth former in the local high school I was mortified to hear his story as editor of the school magazine. He had written an editorial on peace (but not the peace of the official Party line, that is, the Warsaw Pact). Because he had not adopted the Party line he was sent for and questioned by the police after interrogation by the school authorities. He refused to rewrite his editorial. He smiled quietly after telling me this and added: 'Of course, I will not now be going to university'.

I also think of a quite different experience in Istanbul, my first visit to Hagia Sophia.[3] I was almost brought to my knees by the magnificence and ethos of this now somewhat gaunt but deeply moving building. Here was a parable of the fatality of Christian disunity: the sack of Constantinople by the Fourth Crusade, the weakening of Byzantine Christianity, the Fall of Byzantium to the Ottoman Turks, the conversion of the great church into a mosque. And now in a theoretically secular state, the mosque turned into a museum, and yet still one of the great and holy places of Christendom and of the world.

The ecumenism of the future must, of course, take us into dialogue with communities of other faiths. On a visit to the united Churches of North and South India, I visited the shore Temple at Mahabalipuram some miles south of Madras. Inside this temple, right on the shore, carved out of the living rock, there was a representation of the god Vishnu resting on what appeared to be the waters of creation. The Sabbath Rest. It was a deeply moving image of tranquillity after creativity. On the same visit, I spent an afternoon sitting in the courtyard of the old mosque in Delhi and felt once again in a holy place – although of a radically different religious tradition.

Nearer home in more senses than one, I deeply value links with a synagogue in North London through the London Society of Jews and Christians. I remember my first visit to a synagogue many years before, to Bevis Marks, in the City of London itself. I was taken there by my Old Testament tutor as I began to learn Hebrew, an experience never to be forgotten, and in its own way unique even within Judaism, the synagogue maintaining its peculiarly Sephardic traditions.

All these experiences – encounters – which have the power of continuous conversion, are important moments for me on my Christian pilgrimage. They do not replace the necessity for hard theological thought, the careful drafting of statements, the seeming endless theological discussions of ancient themes. There is no short cut. But the ecumenical encounter renews vision and supplies energy and brings one to a living prayer for unity, without which the gift of unity will not be received.

PRAYER

O God of Creation, of the nations and of the Church,
grant to us your pilgrim people the gifts of unity and
peace; that we may be a sign for all humanity of the

*unity which is your will for the whole universe in
Christ: To you be glory in the Church and Christ
Jesus to all generations, for ever and ever. Amen.*

Sentences for discussion

Surprises
I remember my amazement on discovering there were living Nestorians in Ealing.

Lasting holiness
Hagia Sophia ... a parable of the fatality of Christian disunity ... still one of the great and holy places of Christendom.

Renewal through encounter
Encounters – which have the power of continuous conversion, are important moments for me on my Christian pilgrimage. They do not replace the necessity for hard, theological thought, the careful drafting of statements, the seeming endless theological discussions of ancient themes. There is no short cut. But the ecumenical encounter renews vision and supplies energy, and brings one to a living prayer for unity, without which the gift of unity will not be received

NOTES

1. Genesis 28.17.

2. Nestorius, who died in the mid-fifth century, seems to have held that there was both a divine and a human Person in Christ, so that Christ was not one but two Persons. His followers, the Nestorians, continued as a community especially in the region which was once Persia.

3. Hagia Sophia, the great church built by the Roman Emperor Justinian in the 530s in what is now Istanbul.

E. Glenn Hinson

John Loftis Professor of Church History, Richmond Theological Seminary, Richmond, Virginia USA. *Southern Baptist.*

THE FIRST semester I taught Church History at the Southern Baptist Theological Seminary, Louisville, in 1960, I decided to expose the students to the Middle Ages. Where could one do that better than at the Abbey of Gethsemani, a Trappist monastery located about fifty miles from Louisville? Consequently at daybreak on a cool November morning seventy-five Southern Baptist seminarians and I set out on what turned out to be the most rewarding ecumenical venture in our careers.

We were not disappointed in our quest to have an immediate experience of the Middle Ages. The Abbey of Gethsemani still operated in those days just like its forebears at Cîteaux and hundreds of other sites in Europe. Eight times a day the monks trailed one another into the church to chant the Psalms in Latin. Altogether they spent about four hours in the *Opus Dei*, another four in devotional reading and prayer (*lectio divina*) and six hours in manual labor. They ate frugally and, unless sick, only vegetables and fruits. Insofar as we could tell on that quite chilly day, they slept in an unheated dormitory separated only by plywood partitions. Even with our overcoats we shivered as we made our tour of the monastery and were grateful to find the guest house and refectory heated. Under the watchful eye of Father Abbot James Fox the monks dutifully observed the Rule of St Benedict to the letter. For chattery Baptists the silence was awesome. Gethsemani was medieval, centuries from anything any of us had experienced in our lifetimes.

Nothing I had experienced or tried to teach the students had equipped us to make this leap of the centuries. We all had our defenses up. We knew this strange vestige of the past had little to offer us and the people we served. All the

Protestant histories we had read assured us that monasteries were at best relics of a bygone era and at worst wholly irrelevant to intelligent modern Christians. And our visit seemed to confirm all the prejudices we brought with us, that is, until we met Thomas Merton. Merton was an unexpected and wonderful ecumenical surprise.

Merton talked to us about life in the monastery as a life of prayer. When he had finished, he asked if we had any questions. One person whom I feared might do so asked the question I feared someone would ask. It went something like this: 'What is a smart fellow like you doing throwing his life away in a place like this?'

I waited for Merton to open his mouth and eat this guy alive. But he didn't. He just smiled and let love flow out, and he replied, 'I am here because this is my vocation. I believe in prayer.' I could not say what impression this made on all of the students, though time confirmed that it etched itself on their minds and hearts very much as it did on mine. But it bowled me over. You could have knocked me over with a feather. I had never met anyone who believed in prayer enough to consider it a vocation. Indeed, I had heard ministers quote again and again the old cliché, 'God has no hands but our hands, no feet but our feet, no voice but our voice.' Every thump of the tires on the pavement on the way back to the Seminary that evening seemed to drum in my ears, 'You had better hope Merton is right, that prayer does matter enough to spend your life doing it. If the old Protestant rubric is right, this world has to be in a terrible condition.'

Another ecumenical surprise arrived in the mail about two weeks after that visit. I had written a thank you note to the Abbey, but I did not expect to make any further contact for at least a semester. Remembering the rule of silence in the Trappist regimen, I had no thought of making further contact with Thomas Merton and did not know he was corresponding with people all over the world. About two weeks after our visit, therefore, you can imagine my surprise to get a card from Tom saying he would be coming to

Louisville and would like to drop by to see me. Immediately I wrote him. 'Great! How about speaking to my class when you come?' 'I can't speak to groups,' he responded by return mail, 'but if some of my friends happen to be around I can talk to them.' So on a Saturday morning in the fall of 1960 I assembled the entire Faculty of the School of Theology of Southern Seminary, testimony of the ecumenical excitement our first trip to Gethsemani had generated, and we spent two hours talking to Thomas Merton. I can't recall much of the conversation. It doubtless ranged across many fields, for specialists always want to engage others from a point of strength and Merton could beam in on the wave length of other persons in almost any area you wanted to enter. I can recall the impact he made. Here was someone who excited us by his vivacity and by his depth of insight. We knew at once that Roman Catholicism could not be as sinister or as malign as we had been brought up to believe. After our meeting Dale Moody and I drove Tom to this Louisville restaurant, Cunningham's, a 'thirties speakeasy'.

From the fall of 1960 until Merton's untimely death in Bangkok on December 10, 1968 I took students to the Abbey of Gethsemani every semester. In 1965 he began his hermitage and could not meet with the large groups who always wanted to make those visits. During the seven semesters he did host us, he widened the ecumenical horizons of every person who went and generated enthusiasm for ecumenical encounter. When he wrote in the fall of 1965 to tell me he could not meet our group, I concluded that the abbot had imposed some kind of punishment on him for something he had said in a more intimate ecumenical meeting several Louisville ministers had with him in his hermitage. During the latter, Merton conducted a kind of Bible study of Ephesians which eventually steered around to the issue of communion. Dale Moody impulsively interrupted, 'Tom, what is to prevent us from having communion right here?'

96

Merton, never one to weigh every word by canon law, replied without hesitation, 'Nothing. It would not be the Mass. But we could have communion'.

Glancing out of the corner of my eye, I could see that some of the other monks there found that shocking. Later, one took Dale Moody aside to caution that Father Louis often spoke impulsively.

When I got Merton's letter, then, having this incident fresh in mind and unaware how long Merton had tried without success to get permission to be a hermit, I penned a red hot letter to Father Abbot James Fox expressing my dismay that he would throw a monkey wrench into the ecumenical movement by preventing Merton from meeting with us. He had meant so much to our visits in a time when the Second Vatican Council was taking such strides forward, how could the Abbot do such a thing?

Both the Abbot and Merton wrote nice replies and, on our next visit, the Abbot himself hosted us. I learned to admire and respect him immensely as time went on, but he lacked the Merton charisma and communication skills. We kept going, nonetheless, for, through Merton and our earlier visits, we had discovered what drew Merton there and it kept pulling us back and widening our understanding and appreciation for the Roman Catholic Church which birthed both the Trappist order and Thomas Merton.

My own ecumenical journey has taken me a long ways from that first visit to Gethsemani in 1960: membership on the Faith and Order Commission of the World Council of Churches and of the National Council of Churches; Southern Baptist/Roman Catholic Scholars' Dialogues; International Baptist/Catholic Conversations; Consultations with Russian Orthodox in Pyatigorsk in the former USSR; dialogues between Baptists and Episcopalians, Orthodox, Quakers, Lutherans, Pentecostals; hundreds of addresses and exchanges in local, regional, or national gatherings; teaching at Catholic University of America, St John's in Collegeville, Minnesota, and Notre Dame as well as many Protestant colleges, universities, and seminaries. But I doubt whether I would have had such an excursion had it not been for that first visit to Gethsemani. My ecumenical interest antedated that visit, but the unanticipated bonus we received from Thomas Merton energized it and set it on a trajectory which carried far.

The timing was providential. Merton once told me that the fall of 1960 was probably the earliest Gethsemani could have permitted classes such as ours to come to Gethsemani. Behind that, of course, stood the 'New Pentecost' of Pope John XXIII. I have thanked God daily for permitting me to pursue my career as a professor of Church History this side of John XXIII (1958–1963) and the Second Vatican Council (1962–1965). What an ecumenical miracle! In 1988 during one of the International Baptist/Catholic Conversations, which was convened in Rome, Monsignor John A. Radano arranged for us to visit the Scavi under St Peter's. Going through the Scavi is itself a moving experience. But as you come up out of the Scavi, you stand directly in front of the sarcophagus of Pope John XXIII. For me that was one of the most emotional moments of my entire life. Tears flooded my eyes as the reality rushed over me. I could not help but kneel and thank God for the life of this great and good man through whom God was transforming the face of Christendom. Old things were passing away, new were being born because Pope John dared to throw open the windows of the church and let fresh air blow through. And I thanked God for Thomas Merton and the Abbey of Gethsemani, through whom the spirit of John XXIII could reach even the heart of a boy who grew up in the Missouri Ozarks attending the Cave Spring Landmark Missionary Baptist Church, than which none less ecumenical could be found.

PRAYER

*Thank you, O God, for Thomas Mertons who open
our eyes and hearts to a people unknown.
Thank you for Angelo Giuseppe Roncallis,* servi
servorum Dei, *who dare to dream of New Pentecosts.
Thank you for your Church which, through your
Spirit, you renew ever again through the lives of
ordinary saints.
Here is my life, take it and let it be consecrated as
theirs have been to the effecting of* **your** *dream
that all may be One,
Through Jesus Christ, Our Lord. Amen.*

Sentences for discussion

God's plan
The timing was providential. Merton once told me that the
fall of 1960 was probably the earliest Gethsemani could
have permitted classes such as our to come to Gethsemani.

We had discovered what drew Merton there and it kept
pulling us back and widening our understanding and
appreciation for the Roman Catholic Church which birthed
both the Trappist order and Thomas Merton.

I thanked God for Thomas Merton and the Abbey of Gethsemani, through whom the spirit of John XXIII could reach
even the heart of a boy who grew up in the Missouri Ozarks
attending the Cave Spring Landmark Missionary Baptist
Church, than which none less ecumenical could be found.

Rena Karefa-Smart

Ecumenical Officer, Episcopal Church, USA, Diocese of Washington, DC. *African Methodist Episcopal Zion and Episcopal.*

LOOKING BACK and ahead after many years of ecumenical encountering yields a harvest of emotions. Two of these, regret and hope, exist in uneasy tension. Regret over failure of all of our churches to put behind them the scandal of disunity is tempered by the hope that a reunited Church will be a sign of the victory of the transforming power of God in history. What follows are examples of 'living into unity' – or major, personal decisions taken in a changing, tension-filled present which, although uncertain, holds within it the promise of a glorious future of Christians united in and for a world of united communities. 'Keeping hope alive' in a context in which regret is also appropriate requires a long view.

A committed ecumenist, passionately involved in the movement to recover Christian unity, I am resolutely opposed to any effort to compromise the church union focus, to deny the uniqueness and 'finality' of Christian revelation, or to elevate dialogue with other living religions above Christian evangelism. I see connections between the timidity of the churches in the face of such evils as 'Christian' racism, sexism, and 'classism', and the massive suffering which continues in a divided world. I believe that the intransigence of entrenched denominationalism results in divided churches which are painfully impotent before the demons of widespread poverty, war, genocide and environmental decline. Yet it is through the churches that effective ecumenical ministry will prevail. An ecumenical minority exists as a lively presence within the ecumenical movement, living out of a perspective that sees the 'already but not yet' truth of the Church's existence; this minority has shaped my witness, and kept me involved.

Movement toward 'metanoia', a change of heart and direction, began when I was quite young. Christened by water and the Holy Spirit in the African Methodist Episcopal Zion Church, I was a daughter of a Pastor father and a lay leader mother. The Episcopalian organist of our congregation was my godmother. For the first fourteen years of my life, my church experience was of unreconciled diversity – denominational, racial and cultural. Methodist in denomination, defining itself in 'racial' terms, and developing its tradition in a racist context, 'Zion' lived a 'racially' and culturally homogenist existence. I learned early on to work with youth and student colleagues of other denominations. But my experience of church was limited by social history and culture, by the relationships and legacy of slavery and exclusion in which historical Black Methodism developed. Racist conventions in society permitted very little contact with other churches. (Had it not been for the public schools system and the professional and community involvement of my parents in para-church bodies such as Ministers' fraternals and Church Women United I would have had no experience of cross-racial life during my childhood.)

Then when I was fifteen, the Foreign Missions Secretary in our church persuaded my parents to permit me to travel with a party of adults to a world conference of the International Missionary Council in Mexico City. I understood little of the proceedings. But I still remember the vivid liturgies and the cultural and national diversities of the conference participants.

In this way the ecumenical movement came into my life in a church of people I knew, people I was like, and people I loved. In the church I knew, people clung to one another, warmed by the healing and saving power of the known love. For it lighted paths with light that was 'sufficient unto the day' and warmed hearts that would otherwise have grown cold and hard. This church of the people that I knew came into being amidst adversity. It endured, comforting and nurturing its members during great suffering. A 'freedom church', it provided a haven for those who would otherwise have been excluded from membership in the other churches of the period from the late eighteenth century. It developed a tradition of radical and prophetic leadership. Now I was 'surprised by joy' – the joy of discovering churches of people I did not know, of people I am not like, but of people I came to love. Love that was already known in familiar circles became embodied in a diversity truly global. I found that Christians everywhere are gifted with Emmanuel – God with (all of) us. I found that the love of Christ bonds Christians across racial and national and cultural differences in many, many churches.

After my marriage to a physician-minister-ecumenist from Sierra Leone, my home setting became West Africa. I discerned that commitment to the recovery of the gift of Christian unity was now primary in my vocational life. For my heart had changed. I was challenged to respond to the imperative to live Christian unity, whatever that might mean for old denominational loyalties and loves.

The question of denominational affiliation became a burning one. The ecumenical encounter teaches one that wherever Christians stand together, whether at the Holy Eucharist, or before an errant state (as in the struggle against apartheid), there Christ is in power and glory for the redemption of the world. Living this solidarity involves making decisions, hard choices about how to live unity-in-union before churches are fully committed to life in the one Church of Christ. My new family solved the problem of denominational affiliation by addition. Finding no American Methodist Episcopal Zion congregations in Europe or in those parts of Africa where we were often posted, we discovered our affinity with the Anglican Communion. Our decision was not to reject membership in the AME Zion Church, or in the Evangelical United Brethren Church, which was my husband's denomination and also not represented where we lived. We participated in the partner church of our choice in places where there was no AME Zion congregation.

A much more complicated set of considerations formed around my response to my call into Holy Orders. Coming to a clear decision that, since I was called into Holy Orders, I should live out this calling in the two churches in which I had for years been accepted as a lay member in good standing, I requested the only response that seemed to me to be consistent with my ministry. Would the two churches agree to one ordination in which both participated, or to two concurrent ordinations which would be mutually recognised and affirmed in my deployment ? Neither denomination was ready for such an event. I was eventually ordained by each of the denominations independently, two processes that were completed after six years of additional preparation for me, but with no accompanying effort to move the churches along in their journeys into visible unity. I discovered the compassion and support of those in the ecumenical minority.

Although dialogue has begun, and I have been able to minister as an elder (AME Zion) and a priest (Episcopal) for some years now, I live in hope that an ecumenical ministry will be designed by the two churches, and that there will be the opportunity to minister in a manner that is consistent with my ecumenical journey as well as with the conventions of the two churches.

Being encountered and encountering are constitutive of ecumenical formation, whether of persons or of denominations and churches, because we Christians are living in encounter with the Triune God whose will is unity. The matrix in which my identity and self-understanding developed was a tightly spun web of supportive Caribbean and African American family and church relationships. Social history dictated a lived dialectic of subjugation and freedom, contradictory realities that were maintained in problematic tension until I was encountered ecumenically. Then the experience of inclusivity, full participation, and the freedom to choose how to be faithfully Christian opened a new world of possibilities.

To the question, can we Christians ever recover the unity that is the gift of the Holy Spirit – the will of the Triune God in whom we live and move and have our being? my reply continues to be a resounding 'Yes!' The ecumenical movement, through encountering, pushes us into life that leaves no doubt that in time the whole inhabited earth, God's creation, will confess that Jesus Christ is Lord.

PRAYER

Christ our Saviour, Lord of the Church, we humbly thank you that your holy, uniting Spirit is leading us into new paths for the healing of our divisions, that leaders from East and West, North and South, are meeting together in mutual respect and affection, that theologians are finding areas of common ground in ministry and sacraments, that congregations are covenanting with one another in worship prayer, service, and fellowship; that individual Christians are beginning to appreciate and share the treasure of each other's traditions. Grant that our efforts may continue vigorously according to your will until all are one, even as you and the Father are one. Amen

Manual of the Society of the Companions of the Holy Cross (7th ed.) Byfield, Massachusetts, 1984), pp.47–8.

Sentences for Discussion

The churches as instruments
I believe that the intransigence of entrenched denominationalism results in divided churches which are painfully impotent before the demons of widespread poverty, war, genocide and environmental decline. Yet, it is through the churches that effective ecumenical ministry will prevail.

Resolving contradictions
The matrix in which my identity and self-understanding developed was a tightly spun web of supportive Caribbean and African American family and church relationships. Social history dictated a lived dialectic of subjugation and freedom, contradictory realities that were maintained in problematic tension until I was encountered ecumenically.

A new world
Then the experience of inclusivity, full participation, and the freedom to choose how to be faithfully Christian opened a new world of possibilities.

Aram Keshishian

Primate of the Armenian Orthodox Church in the Lebanon and Moderator of the Central Committee of the World Council of Churches. *Oriental Orthodox.*

THE WEEK of Prayer for Christian Unity became the starting point of my ecumenical journey. As a young seminarian in Lebanon in the early 60s, I used to participate together with my classmates in the various activities related to the Week of Prayer for Christian Unity. For the first time in my life I came to witness how people from different churches gather together to pray and reflect together, and seek together the unity of the Church. This very fact of togetherness struck me profoundly. It left a tremendous impact on my life at this early stage of my theological formation. I fell in love with ecumenism, with this 'strange' movement that brings people together in one place and in all places. I started reading ecumenical periodicals with great interest, and following ecumenical news.

As a student, ecumenism was for me a sort of academic interest. As an ordained minister it became a way of life. In other words, the ecumenical movement became the driving force and the sustaining power of my twenty-six years of priestly service. It has remained inseparably interwoven with my reflection and action: simply with my very being. Nobody in fact told me that the ecumenical movement was a movement of the Holy Spirit. I myself discovered it through my own experience. Nobody taught me about the pivotal importance of the ecumenical movement. I myself realized it as I became more and more involved in ecumenical activities. The ecumenical movement is not something to be learned; rather, the Holy Spirit invites us to participate in it with humility and commitment.

I would like to make a few affirmations which emerge out of my relatively limited ecumenical experience.

First, ecumenism is an opening of oneself to the other. We

often realize that as Christians and churches we virtually live in isolation. The historical circumstances and conditions of present day life have isolated us from each other. Sometimes by our own choice we have separated ourselves from others. Ecumenism is essentially the discovery of the other in Jesus Christ, whoever he or she is: black or white, male or female, young or old, ordained or lay person, the one who is created in the image of God and confesses Jesus Christ as Lord and Saviour of the world. I learned in the ecumenical movement how to be critically open towards the other, how to see myself through the eyes of the other. This openness helped me to strengthen and purify my own identity.

Second, ecumenism is an existential dialogue. It is wrong to conceive the ecumenical movement as being exclusively a theological dialogue of theoretical or academic nature and scope. It is a dialogue of people before being a dialogue of ideas, views, perspectives. When the people come together, to think together and to pray together, through that dialogical togetherness, histories, traditions and theologies enter into a dynamic process of creative interaction, which is in fact a source of enrichment and mutual growth.

Third, ecumenism is a learning process. Opening oneself to the other and engaging in dialogue is a serious attempt to know the other as partner. Indeed, how deeply we need to know each other. For many centuries we knew about each other – but so often in a biased, partial and wrong way. The ecumenical movement is a call to know each other, to have a better and greater understanding of each other through joint ventures, common initiatives and close collaboration. How many prejudices, misunderstandings and misinterpretations pertaining to our mutual histories, doctrinal positions and theological teachings have faded away because of ecumenical encounters on local, regional and global levels.

Fourth, ecumenism is a process of mutual challenging. Mutual knowing, learning and sharing is never a passive process. It basically implies mutual critique. The ecumenical movement calls for respect towards each others' positions and traditions. Yet it also calls Christians and churches to grow together by challenging each other and endeavouring to reassess their own identity in Christ *vis-à-vis* the changing realities of human societies.

Fifth, ecumenism is a pilgrimage towards unity. This is the *raison d'être* of the ecumenical movement, and the *sine qua non* condition of any action that claims to be ecumenical. Ecumenism is both a living reminder of our diversity and an urgent call for unity. New priorities of our present day hectic life have almost marginalized the urgency and centrality of unity. I am sure that those people who take part in the ecumenical movement feel so existentially and bitterly the reality of our division. It is in fact this painful experience of disunity that compels people in the ecumenical movement to work together for visible unity.

I learned all these things in the ecumenical movement which became for me a real school. I discovered that we are all Christians – sinful, disobedient, divided – but striving together for full unity. It is remarkable that once you are part of the ecumenical movement, it becomes part of you. Simply, I cannot do without ecumenism.

Prayer is the sustaining and guiding power of the ecumenical movement. Without spirituality, worship and prayer there is no ecumenism. Let us, therefore, in our ecumenical reflection and action, commitment and service, not cease praying to God, holy and eternal Trinity:

PRAYER

To lead us towards communion in faith, life and
  witness;
to sanctify the life of the Church;
to renew its worship and spirituality;
to empower its witness;
and to make visible its unity for his glory and
  kingdom. Amen

Sentences for Discussion

Falling in love with ecumenism

This very fact of togetherness struck me profoundly. It left a tremendous impact on my life at this early stage of my theological formation. I fell in love with ecumenism.

Openness

Ecumenism is an opening of oneself to the other. We often realize that as Christians and churches we virtually live in isolation.

Mutual challenge

Mutual knowing, learning and sharing is never a passive process. It basically implies mutual critique.

Pilgrimage

Ecumenism is a pilgrimage towards unity.

Harding Meyer

Retired, Centre d'Études Oecuméniques, Strasbourg, France.
Lutheran.

I AM 65. I am a Lutheran pastor, and I am an ecumenist. Those three biographical facts, certainly, are not in strict logical relation to one another. Nevertheless, one could at least try to establish some logical linkage. For instance, one could say: he reached the age of 65 in a rather good shape which proves how healthy and rewarding it is to be a Lutheran pastor and, at the same time, an ecumenist. Or: the fact that, although being a Lutheran pastor and 65 years of age, he continues to be an ecumenist is a sign of an almost unconquerable and somewhat un-Lutheran optimism. Let me try a third version: The fact that he is an ecumenist and continues to be even into his sixties, is precisely because he is a Lutheran pastor.

Perhaps none of these versions would amount to sheer nonsense. Probably, each contains a 'grain of truth', a *granum salis*, as we used to say in good academic language.

If I would have to choose among these three versions the least absurd, the one which perhaps contains the biggest 'grain of salt', I would go for the last one: If I am an ecumenist and if I continue to be an ecumenist up to my impending retirement and even beyond, it is precisely because I am a Lutheran pastor.

Indeed, one of the lessons I learned from the fathers of the Wittenberg Reformation is that there is no place for Lutheran complacency and self-centredness. The Lutheran *Magna Carta*,[1] the 'Ausburg Confession',[2] pretends to be, as Melanchthon said in its first Preface, a 'catholic confession', confessing the common apostolic faith and reaching out into the Church catholic, into the *oikoumene*. There is, indeed, a strong and intimate linkage between Lutheranism and ecumenism. But this linkage cannot be taken for granted. Being a Lutheran and being devoted to the ecu-

110

menical cause are by no means always identical. There are, unfortunately, Lutherans who care little about ecumenism. And there are, fortunately, many non-Lutherans who definitely do care.

I confess that I myself really had to learn it. Looking back at my own life as a student and, then, as a teacher of theology, there was a time when I could not have cared less about ecumenism and the unity of the church. Ecumenism, as I understood it at that time, seemed to downplay the quest for truth in favor of the quest for unity.

Events and living experience had to intervene in order to overcome this prejudice and to open my eyes for what should have been obvious to me, i.e., to open my eyes not only to the deep ecumenical intention of the Lutheran Reformation but much more basically to open my eyes to our common Christian confession and common commitment to the oneness of the church in the oneness of faith. And I suppose that most of us who are engaged in the ecumenical endeavor have experienced a comparable, although different existential discovery of ecumenism. I myself can pinpoint almost exactly when and how that happened for me.

In 1958 I started teaching systematic theology at the theological faculty of the Lutheran church in Brazil, a country profoundly shaped by Roman Catholicism in its life and culture, in its customs and language. It happened that, day by day, while lecturing to my students, I could look out of the windows and see on the opposite hill at a mile's distance the large Jesuit College, topped by a huge statue of *Christo Rei*, or 'Christ the King'. I was aware that at the same hour when I was teaching Lutheran students, there, on the opposite hill, Roman Catholic students were taught, both for the same purpose: to be servants of one and the same Christ the King but in churches separated from and even hostile to each other.

During the first months I was not very sensitive to the appalling symbolism of this daily view. I recall that I even used to joke about the fact, that in the valley between the

Lutheran and the Roman Catholic hill, there were the barracks of the Brazilian army, a guarantee for the churches' peaceful coexistence, as we commented ironically.

But this daily demonstration of Christian disunity, this daily view of *Christo Rei* over a kingdom divided in itself and torn apart, became for me and several of my colleagues more and more embarrassing and finally unbearable. We felt that we simply could no longer acquiesce. And already towards the end of the same year there were the first personal contacts with the Jesuit fathers and students, soon followed by regular dialogues on faith and theology which, in 1959, gained momentum by the convocation of the Second Vatican Council.

This was my existential entry into the ecumenical movement, my very personal, if I may say so, 'discovery of ecumenism'. At its centre there was for me the bridging of truth and unity and the growing awareness that the Christian faith must be proclaimed and preserved not by one particular church alone and over against the others, but in the communion of churches.

A couple of years later, I was called to the Lutheran World Federation in Geneva in order to serve, as theological secretary, the ecumenical dialogues world Lutheranism was about to initiate. It was then that my own restricted, narrow and stumbling ecumenical efforts merged with the large and ever broadening stream of Lutheran/Roman Catholic dialogue and its quest for unity in faith.

PRAYER

Jesus Christ, our Lord and our Saviour, we give you thanks that you have received us all together into the great Kingdom of your love. Nothing is stronger than your love; nothing can separate us from it.

We ask you, Lord, let your love be the mother of our love, so that our love for one another might remain lively and not become fatigued, might constantly seek others and not lose sight of them, might be confident and not discouraged, might bear in itself something of the wonderful patience of your love.

Lord, the road to the full unity of your Church is long. We sense this and it often weighs upon us. Who among us will experience the goal? Be with us on this road. Then the goal is not far off and we will be joyful along the way.

Sentences for discussion

Compelling signs

This early demonstration of Christian disunity, this daily view of *Christo Rei* of Christ the King, over a kingdom divided in itself and torn apart, became for me and several of my colleagues more and more embarrassing and finally unbearable.

NOTES

1. This is a reference to the great charter of liberties of early thirteenth century England.

2. The Augsburg Confession of 1530 became for many generations of Lutherans a key statement of position on issues of controversy in the sixteenth century and a defining document of their ecclesial identity.

Maximilian Mizzi

Delegate General for Ecumenism and Interreligious Dialogue, Friars Minor Conventual. Founder of the Franciscan International Centre for Dialogue, Assisi, Italy. *Roman Catholic.*

BEING BORN in a very strong Catholic country, such as the island of Malta, I never had any spiritual relationship with the other Christian communities on the island which were mainly Anglican. Malta was then a British colony and the non-Catholic residents were foreigners. We were very good friends. But when it came to religion we became complete strangers to each other. When we were together we rarely discussed religion. In those times we were not even allowed to go into a non-Roman Catholic church especially during a liturgical service. As a matter of fact, because of the prejudices in which we grew up I had some strange feelings when I passed by one of these churches. I used to think that some very strange things went on in those places.

I entered the Franciscan Order. In 1959 I was transferred to Assisi and became novice master. A few months later, in May 1960, I happened to see two friars wearing a Franciscan habit walking in the main street leading to the Basilica of St Francis. Their habit seemed to me rather strange, and I started to wonder who they were. One of them looked at me. So I said in English 'good morning'. They crossed over to me, and one of the brothers started to tell me what a wonderful experience they had had in Assisi. He also said that they belonged to an Anglican Franciscan community known as the Society of St Francis. I had never heard of that before. He said that they came to the town of St Francis on a spiritual pilgrimage. He also told me that their time in Assisi was over and that the next day they were going back to England. Both of the Brothers spoke with enthusiasm about St Francis and about their stay in Assisi. We also talked a little bit about the forthcoming Second Ecumenical Vatican Council. They said they were looking forward to it with great hope. Before we left each other they invited me to their house in England.

This meeting remained vivid in my mind. Every now and then we wrote to each other. Then some time after, during the Week of Prayer for Christian Unity, we exchanged incense to be used during our services in the Basilica of St Francis and in the chapel of the Mother House of the Society of St Francis in Dorset, England. After that I started to meet a number of British people belonging to the Anglican church while on their pilgrimage to Assisi. I showed them around the Basilica of St Francis and other Franciscan shrines. We never prayed together, though it did not take too long before that too happened. We were still before Vatican II, and the word 'ecumenism' was not known to any of us. But I was already wondering why we should not pray together.

One evening one of these Anglican groups asked me to dinner at the Guest House of the Franciscan Sisters of the Atonement where they were lodged. A very friendly group conversation followed during which we talked about our churches and about our traditions. The evening ended with some night prayers and Compline. At this point I thought that I should not leave. It was my first ecumenical prayer, which I felt was very deep.

The meeting with the Anglican Franciscans near the Basilica of St Francis in Assisi which seemed to be just casual was the beginning of a very important ecumenical movement in Assisi focused around the Basilica of St Francis which is the burial place of the saint of peace and reconciliation. What seemed to be casual proved to be a part of God's plan where Christians belonging to different Christian confessions and religions gather together in love, respect, prayer and reconciliation.

With the ecumenical Second Vatican Council ecumenism in Assisi started to take a more official and organised shape. Soon after the Vatican Council some Lutherans from Sweden and Denmark found their way to Assisi attracted both by the spirituality of St Francis and by the ecumenical activities that were being carried out.

One day I met some of these people. It was another new experience and inspirational to all of us. Little by little many more people from Scandinavia started to visit Assisi for ecumenical reasons. Since then thousands of Lutherans from Northern Europe have been visiting Assisi. During these visits we have regular ecumenical services, dialogue, meditations and prayers. The ecumenical spirit soon spread to many parts of Scandinavia, especially in Sweden and in Denmark.

One thing leads to another. Some years ago a young woman from Denmark belonging to the Lutheran tradition came on a few days' visit to Assisi with some of her friends. Some of these had stopped practising their Christian faith and resorted to practising non-Christian Eastern religions. Their visit to Assisi and our meeting with each other gave both them and me some thoughts for reflection. The visit to the town of St Francis made them rediscover their Christian heritage. Now in Denmark as well as in Sweden there is a strong ecumenical movement which takes its inspiration from the Franciscan tradition.

I believe that one very important factor in this process has been my willingness to meet people on a friendly basis, to talk with people, to listen to others and to try to help people, regardless of creed, race or nationality. In this process I think it is most important to be open and to set aside any fear of being overwhelmed by what others might say or do. This attitude has helped me to face people belonging to different Christian traditions and to different religions on an equal basis. In meeting people of other faiths I have always felt that I should be positive rather than negative with them. Very often I remembered what Pope John XXIII once said that is to take first into consideration those things that we have in common rather than to concentrate on those things which separate us. This I found very helpful when, later, I started to meet people belonging to other religions.

Without minimizing the importance of the theological dialogue and the work of the theological commissions between the churches, I believe that grassroot-level ecumenism is of the utmost importance. If this is neglected it will be much more difficult to break down the psychological barriers and the prejudices which have been created during centuries of conflict and misunderstanding. More often than not those in the street have fewer mental restrictions to prevent them accepting the theological truth than some theologians. This is a common experience in our daily life ecumenism in Assisi. Unfortunately this sort of grass-root-level ecumenism does not find enough room in many churches. It would be very helpful if this were encouraged and fostered.

One more very important factor in this sort of ecumenism is the fact that when people from different Christian confessions come together they very often spend some time praying together. And prayer is the most important means of achieving Christian unity.

In 1973 a delegation of Buddhist monks from Laos visited Assisi. I felt no objection to arranging a short service of prayer at the tomb of St Francis. I felt that it was good that such things could happen. It was a completely new experience for me, which led to many other interreligious meetings on a spiritual basis.

In November of 1978 Pope John Paul II made his first pilgrimage to the Basilica of St Francis. That was only a few days after his election to the See of Peter. On that occasion he prayed at the tomb of St Francis and addressed the thousands of people that gathered around the Basilica. Before he left Assisi he had an informal and friendly meeting with the Franciscan community in the large refectory of the *Sacro Convento*. On that occasion I felt bold enough to talk to the Pope about our ecumenical and interreligious activities, and presented him with an album of photos and cuttings from papers illustrating these activities. The Pope showed a great interest in these things. A few days later I received a letter of thanks from the Secretary of State of the Vatican on behalf of Pope John Paul II, who also gave his blessing on this work.

On October 27, 1986 the Pope came to Assisi to pray for

peace with representatives of nearly all the religions of the world. That meeting reminded me of the short talk I had with the Pope in 1978 on his first visit. I had a feeling that he might well have been inspired in some remote way by that short conversation and illustration of what had been going on in Assisi for so many years.

That big meeting in Assisi of the Pope and the world's religions has been called a 'prophecy of peace'. Pope John Paul II always refers to it as the 'spirit of Assisi'. This has opened the way to lots of similar meetings all over the world. I truly believe that the meeting in Assisi of October 27, 1986, can be rightly called a prophetic gesture. It may be that not even the Pope himself had realised then the great impact that that meeting would have on the world's religions. That prayer meeting of religions started a new process which brings with it new theological, spiritual, ecumenical, interreligious and social attitudes. As Christian and Franciscan, I strongly believe that this is the work of the Holy Spirit. I also like to think that the church and the religions of the world have started to walk together towards the one, true God in whom they will all be united some day.

PRAYER

Lord Jesus, you founded your church on earth as a
sign of your Father's love for the human race. You
founded this community on love, in one faith and in
one baptism. As time passed by we neglected your
commandment to love one another as you love us and
to be one as you and your Father are one. We have
sinned against you and against each other by
breaking our harmony with you and with one
another. For this we repent and ask your forgiveness.
Lord Jesus send your Holy Spirit upon your
Church to make it holy and in your love and mercy
gather all your children in love and in the same one
baptism, in the same one faith that you transmitted
to your apostles.

*Make your church a sign of your presence in the
world so that the world may believe in you.
Lord make me an instrument of your peace and
reconciliation. Amen.*

Sentences for discussion

God's plan
The meeting with the Anglican Franciscans near the
Basilica of St Francis in Assisi which seemed to be just
casual was the beginning of a very imporant ecumenical
movement in Assisi focussed around the Basilica of St
Francis which is the burial place of the saint of peace and
reconciliation. What seemed to be casual proved to be a
part of God's plan where Christians belonging to different
Christian confessions and religions gather together in love,
respect, prayer and reconciliation.

Prayer
Prayer is the most important means of achieving Christian
unity.

Openness
I believe one very important factor ... has been my willingness to meet people on a friendly basis ... In this process I
think it is most important to be open and to set aside any
fear of being overwhelmed by what others might say or do.
This attitude has helped me to face people belonging to different Christian traditions and to different religions on an
equal basis.

Grassroots ecumenism
Without minimizing the importance of theological dialogue
and the work of the theological commissions between the
churches I believe that grassroot level ecumenism is of the
utmost importance.

Walter G. Muelder

Dean and Professor of Social Ethics, Emeritus, Boston University School of Theology, Boston, Massachusetts, USA. *United Methodist.*

The Formative Process

I early developed a spirit and habit of inclusiveness in a German Methodist parsonage, in the secular atmosphere of public schools in Peoria and San Jose, Illinois, in high school and junior college in Burlington, Iowa, followed by attendance at Knox College (Galesburg, Illinois) with its nondenominational Christian ambience. While at Knox, I was assigned a student pastorate for two small churches. For these I had weekly sermon preparation and drew heavily on current articles in *The Christian Century*, the books of Harry Emerson Fosdick, Sherwood Eddy, Kirby Page, Tolstoy, Gandhi, as well as on the world's great literature as interpreted in this fine liberal arts college from which I graduated at age 20 in 1927.

I decided for the Methodist Ministry and enrolled in Boston University School of Theology. Training there was supplemented by the rich content and stimulation of many mainline Boston pulpits, the Community church, a brief responsibility in a Congregational church and a two-year Methodist student pastorate.

I was fully ordained in 1931. The previous year I spent at the University of Frankfurt in Germany, where I studied principally under Paul Tillich. I then enrolled for doctoral studies in philosophy under Edgar S. Brightman at Boston University. Brightman's philosophy of religion stressed both personal idealism and the empirical coherence of truth. The above studies, together with research on Ernst Troeltsch's philosophy of history, which was the subject of my Ph. D. dissertation, rounded out my formal education. When I began to teach at Berea College at age 27, I was an ordained Methodist minister, a democratic socialist, a pacifist, and a philosopher/theologian dedicated to the spirit of

Christian unity. During my final two years as a graduate student I was a student-pastor of a Congregational Church in New Hampshire whose polity differed from that of episcopal Methodism. Working in contrasting institutions was invaluable.

Academically-based Ecumenism

Like Knox College, Berea was nondenominational. Its crest, 'God has made of one blood all nations', reflected its early interracial origins. It was dedicated to serving the poor of Appalachia. President William J. Hutchins charged me as Professor of Bible and Philosophy with the ecumenical task: 'to build a golden bridge' from the varieties of sectarian Biblical literalism that characterized Southern Appalachia in those days, to the modern world. Most of the faculty belonged to Union Church, which affiliated itself directly with the Federal Council of Churches. Accordingly, as a church we were deeply interested in the work of the Oxford and Edinburgh Conferences of 1937. I was also the adviser of the student YMCA and served on the Southeast Regional Field Council, an interracial body which cooperated with the student YWCA and was related through the national organizations to the World Student Christian Federation. I was also active in the Fellowship of Reconciliation, the Socialist Party, and the Conference of Southern Churchmen. While at Berea I became a Fellow of the National Council on Religion in Higher Education.

In 1940 I was called to teach Christian theology and Christian ethics at the Graduate School of Religion of the University of Southern California. Hardly any greater contrast in religion and culture can be found in the USA than moving from Appalachia to Los Angeles. In Los Angeles I continued my heavy involvement in the Student Christian Movement; and when the Second World War broke out I lectured extensively in churches of many denominations on issues of the war and post-war reconstruction, such as the evacuation of persons of Japanese ancestry, the plight of German exiles, labor problems in the war industries, conscientious objection to the war, post-war planning, and race relations. I also became co-chairperson of the Commission on Race Relations of the Los Angeles Church Federation and Chairman of the Albert Schweitzer Fellowship whose mission was to supply his hospital with medicines. I was active in the secular ecumenism of the Council for Civic Unity, the Civil Liberties Union and projects of the American Friends Service Committee. My classes at the University reflected the pluralism of Los Angeles Protestant churches and the need for unity.

Boston and Conciliar Ecumenism

My move to Boston University School of Theology as Dean and Professor of Social Ethics in 1945 went with a rapid development in 'conciliar' ecumenism. This involved me with the Massachusetts Council of Churches in matters of church-state relations, the Federal Council of Churches in economic ethics, and the World Council of Churches on many fronts. In due course I also participated in the Consultation on Church Union, in full session as an Observer at the Second Vatican Council and in leading in the organizing of the Boston Theological Institute, now a consortium of nine theological seminaries in the Boston area.

The period from 1945 to 1975 had two major dimensions, one related to conciliar activity and the other to developments within Boston University. For a number of years I served on the Federal Council's Commission on the Church and Economic Life. Then came the National Council's cooperation with Boston University in an annual Summer Institute of Ecumenism. At the World Council level I participated first on the Committee of Twenty-five (1951–54) in writing the report on the theme of the Evanston Assembly, 'Jesus Christ, the Hope of the World.' In 1952 I was appointed to the Faith and Order Commission and served until 1975. In 1953 I taught a full semester at the Graduate School of the Ecumenical Institute at the Chateau de Bossey. From 1954 to 1961 I was co-chairperson of the Department on the Cooperation of Men and Women in Church and Society. At the New Delhi Assembly (1961) I was appointed chairperson of the Board of the Ecumenical Institute. In 1968 I was a Methodist delegate at Uppsala, my third responsibility at an Assembly.

Meanwhile a special responsibility came in 1956 when the Faith and Order Commission asked me to chair a commission to study the non-theological factors that inhibit unity in the churches. With Nils Ehrenstrom as secretary we produced *Institutionalism and Church Unity* for the World Conference on Faith and Order (Montreal, 1963),

My special interests in Christian social ethics were expressed in preparation for the 1966 Conference on Church and Society, an essay on 'Theology and Social Science,' which appeared in John C. Bennett, ed., *Christian Social Ethics in a Changing World*. My last Faith and Order meeting was in Accra in 1974. In 1978 I wrote 'A Cooperative Study of Twenty-One North American Churches on Church Unity.'

At Boston University the Summer Institute ran from 1951 to 1970. Nils Ehrenstrom was appointed as the first full-time professor of Ecumenics in any theological seminary. In addition, the faculty of the School of Theology encouraged student enrolment at the Graduate School of the Ecumenical Institute and awarded a full semester's credit. The Boston Theological Institute was established; I was the first president. This is now more than a quarter-century old as a thriving ecumenical consortium.

A long life as ecumenist

Since formal retirement in 1972 I have continued to teach, having completed as of 1993/94 sixty consecutive years in the field. I serve on ad hoc committees of the Massachusetts Council of Churches and in the Social Ethics Group of the Boston Theological Institute. In 1985 I was presented the Forrest Knapp Ecumenical Award by the Massachusetts Council of Churches.

123

PRAYER

*O blessed Trinity, grant that the unity we seek in
Thy holy Church may be the unity which you bless.
We confess our shameful divisions and our blindness
to inclusive truth. The vision of the unity we have in
Christ makes us painfully aware of the scandal of
continuing separation among our churches. We
remain introverted in our loyalties to our diverse
institutional practices, confusing the things that are
human devices with divine ordinances. We often
make of our traditions idols of loyalty. Therefore we
pray for humility and purity of heart that we both see
and do the tasks that belong to our common
pilgrimage.*

*Grant to us, O precious Christ, the love that finds
community in service, courage in pursuing social
justice, and respect for worthy diversity. May we not
grow weary in serving the ecumenical movement.
May we indeed do all things together except those
which in conscience we cannot do in Thee. Help us
so to act that the closer we draw to Thee the closer we
are drawn to one another as persons and
communions.*

*May Thy Holy Spirit empower us to break through
the sinful barriers of our resistance to that unity
which rightly serves the coming of the realm of God.
Amen*

Sentences for discussion

Bridge-building

President William J. Hutchins charged me as Professor of
Bible and Philosophy with the ecumenical task:' to build a
golden bridge' from the varieties of sectarian Biblical literalism that characterized Southern Appalachia in those
days, to the modern world.

Cormac Murphy-O'Connor

Bishop of Arundel and Brighton, England, and Roman Catholic
Co-Chairman of ARCIC II. *Roman Catholic.*

ONE DAY, as I was sitting in my study in the Venerable
English College, Rome, where I was then Rector, I received
a telephone call from the Rector of the Pontifical Gregorian
University, which my students frequented for their studies.
He asked me if I would offer hospitality to an English
Minister of the United Reformed Church who was due to
give a series of lectures on ecumenism at the University. I
said I would be very pleased to do so.

It was then that Dr Norman Goodall came into my life.
He resided at the English College for one whole term, and
what extraordinarily happy weeks we spent together.
Norman had an outstanding facility for entering into the
lives and interests of other people and, in this case, especially the young students at the college. He entered into
their world as if it were second nature to him, and he
described this in the following way: 'We talked about
heaven and hell as easily as about cabbages and kings,
about the world in which we live and the world we are
made for; about life's delights and absurdities, and most of
all about those centralities of the faith and the experience of
grace in which is our real and unassailable unity'. I con-
ceived a very great admiration and affection for Norman
during those months that we spent together. We talked,
laughed, prayed and shared so many things. Strange, is it
not, how a common sense of humour brings people together, and this Norman and I had. But beneath it all there
was the consciousness of a shared reality of life in Christ.
We could as easily pray together as make music together; as
easily talk about God as talk about the literature we
enjoyed. These were very precious months. I found that my
meeting and friendship with Norman was the beginning of
a new insight into what ecumenism really meant.

Norman returned to the College a year later and we continued to keep in touch from time to time until I left Rome and became Bishop of Arundel and Brighton. I recall now the last time I had occasion to meet him. I was driving back from Birmingham to Sussex and I decided on the spur of the moment that I would make a detour to see Norman at his home in Oxford. He was very weak and we were so glad to see each other again. We talked about our friendship, about God's forgiveness and love, and then, on parting, we blessed each other. Two days later he died.

For me, Norman Goodall marked a new path on my ecumenical journey. He reminded me that our shared life in Christ, through our common baptism, is more important than any aspects of disunity that we still have to bear. He reminded me that ecumenism is first of all a meeting together, and out of friendship and affection come desires for a deeper unity which the Holy Spirit inspires within our hearts. Finally, Norman Goodall exemplified for me the truth that ecumenism, as has been said, is not just 'about the removal of obstacles but about the sharing of gifts'. Norman and I shared what gifts we had together and acknowledged them as gifts of God. Norman was one manifestation of the manifold gifts of God in my life. I pray that, as Thomas More said, 'We may merrily meet in heaven'.

PRAYER

Lord Jesus Christ, you said to your apostles: I leave
you peace, my peace I give you. Look not on our sins
but on the faith of your Church and grant us the
peace and unity of your kingdom where you live for
ever and ever. Amen.

Sentences for discussion

Ecumenical friendship
We could as easily pray together as make music together; as easily talk about God as talk about the literature we

enjoyed. These were very precious months. I found that my meeting and friendship with Norman was the beginning of a new insight into what ecumenism really meant.

Norman and I shared what gifts we had together and acknowledged them as gifts of God. Norman was one manifestation of the manifold gifts of God in my life. I pray that, as Thomas More said, 'We may merrily meet in heaven'.

William A. Norgren

Retired Ecumenical Officer, The Episcopal Church in the United States of America, New York, USA. *Anglican.*

WE HEARD in General Theological Seminary about the World Conference on Faith and Order at Lund (1952) from a professor who was there. But my first personal ecumenical influence came at the Patristic Conference in Oxford in the late 1950s when a renowned Roman Catholic patristic scholar's lecture was introduced by the Archbishop of Canterbury, Dr Geoffrey Fisher. The unity of the Church was still there even after centuries of estrangement. This symbolic act contrasted with the rivalries I witnessed between Anglicans and Roman Catholics at the university.

But soon John XXIII's announcement of the Second Vatican Council helped illuminate the meaning of this event. We learned later that leading Anglican and Roman Catholic theologians had been meeting quietly during the pontificate of Pope Pius XII. The Church of England had become aware of theological trends in the Roman Catholic Church and wished to become better informed about them.

Upon returning to the USA I was surprised when asked if I would be interested in the new position of director of Faith and Order Studies in the National Council of Churches. One recommendation of the North American Conference on Faith and Order at Oberlin (1957) was to bring Faith and Order work into the Council, whose work until then focused on activities in the ecumenical movement such as social witness, evangelism, stewardship, communication, education, overseas mission. This was seen as a challenge for a younger theologian and the Council appointed me. One of my first tasks was to attend World Council of Churches meetings at Spittal, Austria where the gathering of Christian leaders from around the world gave concrete expression to the *oikoumene* and afforded a great deal of information. At home Faith and Order began with a committee of communion representatives headed by Dr James I. McCord, president of Princeton Theological Seminary. We began a study of the 'Ecclesiological Significance of Councils of Churches', continued with 'Order and Organisation', and similar projects followed. These involved some of the most seasoned theologians and leaders in the nation.

In 1959 during an assembly of the National Council of Churches, Eugene Carson Blake proposed in Grace Cathedral, San Francisco, that the Episcopal Church and the United Presbyterian Church invite the Methodist Church and the United Church of Christ to form a united Church in the USA on the model of Church Unions in India, Bangladesh and Pakistan. His vision was comprehensive: of a Church catholic and reformed. His explanation of 're-formed' included the ideas of continuing reformation, democratic process and laity participation. His explanation of 'catholic' was in terms of the Anglo-Catholic practices and understandings within the Episcopal Church. Blake's vision was indeed comprehensive; my conversation with him indicated he saw this as a step in the direction of an eventual wider union, including the Orthodox churches. Before the Second Vatican Council it was inconceivable that the churches would in future give so much attention to unity with the Roman Catholic Church. In the light of his governing vision, it is curious that the media afterward developed the habit of describing the Consultation as though it had seen its way in exclusively Protestant terms. The proposal evoked a response and led to the Consultation on Church Union.[1] Discussions of an organizational and governmental union did not succeed and led to discussions of an alternative model of covenant communion.

It became clear to National Council leadership that the Second Vatican Council would be an ecumenical milestone, as well as important for the renewal of the Church. Cardinal Augustin Bea visited National Council and denominational leaders in New York City (at the Morgan house headquarters of the Lutheran Church in America). I was assigned as a 'guest observer' and participated in each of the last three sessions for several months. This was another gathering of church leaders from around the world: bishops and theologians as well as official Orthodox, Protestant and Anglican observers. The observers joined in a new way in the struggle to interpret and decide on ecclesiological, Church-world, ecumenical, interfaith, religious liberty, and other matters which were being discussed. The 'separated brethren' listened and learned, and made clear their positions on the same matters.

There were at least two important consequences at home. The first was an awareness of the implications of Council decisions for both Roman Catholics and 'separated brethren'. That led to the book, *Living Room Dialogues*, for lay discussion groups, promoted by dioceses and Councils of Churches across America. The second was the perception of the need for Faith and Order studies to be more inclusive. This led to the formation of a wider Faith and Order Forum to include participants from the National Conference of Catholic Bishops, the Lutheran Church-Missouri Synod, Southern Baptist Convention, and certain conservative evangelical churches. Roman Catholics were seconded to the Faith and Order staff, including Father David Bowman, S. J. and Sister Ann Ware. This was a further reflection of the good relations through ecumenical officer Monsignor William Baum, later Archbishop of Washington and a cardinal in Rome.

My service in the National Council ended after twelve years, and I worked in the weekday ministry of Trinity Parish, New York City. Here I learned much about ministry to and with the four hundred thousand persons who move into the downtown area daily, ministry which is by no means limited to Episcopalians. The outreach of congregations in our communions is wider than we often suppose. The ecumenical movement brought to people in most communions (not yet all) a sense of Christian friendship based ultimately on their common baptismal faith.

After three years I was called again to specialized ecumenical work in 1975, by Presiding Bishop John M. Allin in the Ecumenical Office of the Episcopal Church. In partnership with other Anglican Provinces, the Episcopal Church participates in world dialogues with the Orthodox, Oriental Orthodox, Roman Catholic and Lutheran Churches, and less frequently with the Reformed and Methodist churches. In the USA, there are parallel dialogues with the first four, and in the context of the Consultation on Church Union, conversations with the Methodist, Reformed, and Disciples of Christ churches. As a whole, these dialogues have been startlingly productive of agreements, but it is a more difficult and complex matter for the people of the churches to 'receive' the agreements – at least quickly – in the life of their churches.

Significantly, it is the theological community which 'powers' the dialogues, and their agreements give strength to fragile local ecumenical work and help us stay together with confidence. Yet the agreements encounter resistance from the corporate memory and within the institutional life of the churches, and the ecumenical vision of church leaders is often not shared by other leaders, who are preoccupied with special demands of their jobs. This suggests that ecumenical formation should focus on actual and emerging intermediate leaders, whether laity, seminarians, or clergy.

In the 1970s, ecumenical officers in Episcopal[2] dioceses banded together to form a national ecumenical network called Episcopal Diocesan Ecumenical Officers (EDEO). Responsible for sharing local ecumenical projects and responding to the dialogues and other national and international initiatives, the network has constituted a major expansion of ecumenical leadership. Even learnings from important international assemblies of the World Council of Churches can be communicated through the network. Still, ecumenical learning belongs to the total mission of the Church, to all the people. Church leaders must work out the means by which limited resources can be used to prepare people for the full expression of *koinonia* (communion) in the Holy Eucharist. The gospel of reconciliation with justice and the tradition of the great Church, cannot be hidden from the world which awaits it. The revealing of the visible unity of the Church is on its way, and I am pleased to have a part in it.

This has been a story of corporate work, not only personal experience. Yet, I believe it also tells a story about points of encounter for others, past and potential.

PRAYER

O God of peace, who through thy Son Jesus Christ didst set forth one faith for the salvation of humankind: Send thy grace and heavenly blessing upon all Christian people who are striving to draw nearer to thee and to each other, in the unity of the Spirit and in the bond of peace. Give us penitence for our divisions, wisdom to know thy truth, courage to do thy will, love which shall break down the barriers of prejudice and pride, and an unswerving loyalty to thy holy Name. Unite us all in thee as thou, O Father, with thy Son and the Holy Spirit, art one God, world without end. Amen.[3]

Sentences for discussion

New generations
This suggests that ecumenical formation should focus on actual and emerging intermediate leaders, whether laity, seminarians, or clergy.

Common baptism
The ecumenical movement brought to people in most communions (not yet all) a sense of Christian friendship based ultimately on their common baptismal faith.

WILLIAM A. NORGREN

NOTES

1. This began in 1962, following the initiative of Eugene Carson Blake, the Stated Clerk of the United Presbyterian Church in the USA and Bishop James A. Pike of the Episcopal Church in the United States of America. By the time it was launched it included an enlarged body of churches, and it has gone on to reflect the changing thinking of the ecumenical movement in its purposes.

2. That is, dioceses of the Episcopal Church in the United States of America.

3. Bishop Anderson, Faith and Order Manual (1927).

Mercy Amba Oduyoye

Deputy General Secretary, World Council of Churches. *Methodist.*

MY ECUMENICAL journey has not been an interior one. It has been a matter of participating in the movement as opportunities presented themselves. It is a simple straight-forward story of responding to calls. I was past thirty before I set foot anywhere outside Ghana, but inside Ghana, I had travelled the country from the farthest north to its coastline and lived in seven different locales of varying cultures. I did not know the word 'ecumenical', but looking back I feel I was prepared during this period to appreciate different styles of life and ways of doing things.

My first ecumenical experience took place at school. Achimota secondary school was a government school, at a time when most secondary schools were church schools; but on any particular week day the students, all boarding, had a choice of three places to spend the first half hour of the school timetable. They were the school chapel, the detention room or the Roman Catholic service held in the music school. I had no idea until much later that communion services at the school chapel where all who were not Roman Catholics went, were in fact High Church Anglican. It made no difference when I, a Methodist, came to discover this and it still makes no difference to me. The formal theological education I had in the universities of Ghana and Cambridge bore no particular denominational stamp, neither did the informal one through the Student Christian Movement. But one does not escape the spirituality of a Methodist upbringing.

Christian presence

My ecumenical journey proper began when I was called at short notice to help on the host committee of a World Student Christian Federation (WSCF) conference held at the University of Ghana, Legon, in the fall of 1965, on

'Christian Presence in the Academic World'. When you are brought up in a Methodist Manse, when asked to do something for the church you just do it. So giving my time to the WSCF was natural.

I had just returned from a two-year study of dogmatics at Cambridge University in England, during which I had been sustained by regular attendance at Wesley Chapel, and an occasional appearance at Great St Mary's, the Anglican Church (which at that time was featuring lectures by J.A.T. Robinson on 'The Death of God'). During one vacation I joined a group of Roman Catholic students to share church and student life in Holland and kept in touch with my host family in Arnheim for a long time. Other vacations were spent with a Methodist family in Colne, Lancashire.

I felt happy to be back on familiar territory. Legon Hall Chapel was 'simply Protestant', or was it really Anglican? It did not matter, it was 'all Christians together', and everyone behaved in a very Methodist way by being keenly concerned with social justice and Scriptural holiness. We were young people whose Christian life was made up of worshipping, witnessing and working. Legon added to my growth in ecumenical living. The Department of Theology (later of the Study of Religions), where I studied, had a Roman Catholic, a Methodist, a Presbyterian, a couple of Anglicans and a Muslim on its faculty.

I remember talking to the Reverend Adeolu Adegbola about career plans and eliminating firmly any call to the ministry. Imagine my surprise when in the plenary of the 1965 conference he stood up to talk about me. Of course he did not mention my name and I do not remember all that he said, except one thing that stuck in my mind because it was so true: 'We have right here a young woman who just came back from theological studies in Cambridge and neither church nor university knows what to do with her'. Well, today I understand the problem my choice of studies and my arrival on the scene in that particular year caused the very people who had promoted my theological studies. To be posted to Wesley Girls' High School to teach literature in English and Bible study up to the sixth form was a challenge and a delight, and I have it on good authority that this was so from the perspective of the girls in my class.

School teaching lasted only two years, for unknown to me, Adegbola's speech followed by a long walk and conversation with Albert van den Heuvel was leading to an ecumenical appointment for me. Adegbola was 'chairman' of the Youth Committee of the World Council of Churches (WCC), and van den Heuvel was Director of the Youth Department. Neither had said anything in Legon about working in Geneva, but in 1966 I had an invitation to a consultation on Christian education and ecumenical commitment jointly sponsored by the World Council of Christian Education (WCCE) and the World Council of Churches. The meeting was held at Boldern, near Zurich (Switzerland).

When this was followed by another invitation to a WCCE conference in Nairobi, one of my colleagues at Wesley Girls High School, a British woman, a self-declared agnostic, with whom I shared the preparatory papers, said after a long silence: 'It will not take long before we see you heading this World Council of Churches'. Well, I did not. But in 1967 I went to work as Youth Secretary in the WCC Youth Department, jointly appointed by the WCC/WCCE. The latter was preparing its integration into the WCC. Twenty years later I returned to the WCC as a Deputy General Secretary and Staff Moderator of the Unit on Education and Renewal. With a reorganisation that took effect January 1992 I became Deputy General Secretary (Programme Planning and Coordination). From 1970 when I left the Youth Department till 1987 when I returned to the General Secretariat I never left the World Council of Churches.

Serving as a teacher, whether at school or university, was for me exercising a ministry of Christian presence. This has become the prism through which I see the ecumenical movement. It is an aspect of the churches together witnessing to the love of God and facilitating the witness of other Christian movements. This joint witness for me is what demonstrates the churches' unity.

Ecumenical service

Ecumenical service is not limited to staff positions. Indeed many more serve the movement as volunteers, and I have been part of this growing family of the promoters of ecumenism. From the Youth Department of the WCC I joined the All Africa Conference of Churches (AACC) as Youth Secretary working from Ibadan. It was during this period that together with Aaron Tolen and Jose Chipenda I organised the second All Africa Youth and Students Conference held at Ibadan and tried to promote joint work through a consultative group which we formed to guide the work of the WSCF (Africa) and the Youth Department of the AACC. Being AACC Youth Secretary meant that I was in touch with the WCC Youth Committee and also with the International Christian Youth Exchange. Somehow or other, between my first international ecumenical meeting of September 1967 and when I returned to the WCC staff, there has been hardly a year in my life without an ecumenical encounter. I even served as President of the World Student Christian Federation, the first woman to have had that responsibility.

I had left the WCC for AACC to be based in Ibadan because Modupe and I had got married. He was working in Ibadan as General Secretary of the Student Christian Movement (SCM) in Nigeria. Then, faced with the choice of moving to Nairobi in order to stay in the service of AACC, I opted out of AACC which had taken a decision to centralise its offices and so was closing down the Ibadan office. Back I went to teaching the Bible and literature in English, this time in a boys' school.

Lagelu Grammar School was for me quite an experience. Unlike Bodija Estate, where I lived, the ecumenical congregation I attended in Jericho (former white reservation), and the company of SCM senior friends, Lagelu was a Yoruba community. Because it was a community school there were both Christians and Muslims. At my first Friday assembly I stood aghast while the whole Assembly led by one of the students broke into a prayer in Arabic; it was an Islamic prayer. That was my first experience of 'praying in each other's presence'. More impressive is the testimony of a Muslim lad to whom I taught the Bible. Meeting me later in life he said: 'I enjoyed Bible knowledge, especially when you taught so much about justice'. He remains a Muslim. There, without any intentional ecumenical formation, this young man acquired a very important perspective for inter-religious relations. Like him, I had learned that all religious people have to join in promoting what humanises human-ity. In many such informal ways I have shared my ecu-menical convictions, especially that of the unity of the Church of Christ and the need to live and witness as one Church and to respect the humanity of the people we encounter.

I have been privileged to be present at four WCC Assem-blies, two (Uppsala, Canberra) as WCC staff and two (Nairobi, Vancouver) as church delegate. I participated in the WCC Mission Conference in Bangkok and the WSCF Assembly in Colombo. I have participated at various levels in the work of WCC's Faith and Order Plenary Com-mission, Standing Commission, smaller working consulta-tions and in the World Conference at Santiago de Compostela (Spain), which followed that of Montreal with a gap of thirty years. Since 1977 I have been a member of the Ecumenical Association of Third World Theologians, and shared in the efforts to promote a living theology.

For me this has meant a theology that is relevant to Africa and which includes women's reflections and concerns. It is in this connection that I stimulated the creation of The Circle of Concerned African Women Theologians to re-search and write on the issues and challenges of women in religion and culture.

Participation in several Church and ecumenical women's meetings in North America, Europe, Asia, New Zealand and Africa has assured me of the basic unity of women's issues and the reality of women's solidarity worldwide. I have witnessed the struggle to move from presence through participation to partnership. I have participated in and spoken at many ecumenical meetings of young people and others of mixed groups, and those organised by national and local churches. In most of these my assignment has been to provide an input on theology, the Church's mission, issues affecting women and young people or their contributions to creative developments.

The challenge of unity

One of the most memorable ecumenical encounters which caused me to reflect for days, and still challenges my participation, happened in the United States. In the 1970s an ecumenical encounter was organised there to challenge the United States' involvement in the Vietnam war. After the convocation those of us present as international guests were sent two by two to visit a number of churches for the purpose of sharing the results of the meeting, and to witness against the war in Vietnam. At one church, after I had spoken on the theme of the need to put an end to the war in Vietnam, a hand shot up from the back during question time; it was that of a white man in his late 40s: 'Did you say you come from Nigeria?' he queried. I responded in the affirmative. Though Ghanaian I was at the time living in Nigeria, having gone to join my spouse just after the Nigerian civil war. 'How can you come here to tell us to get out of Vietnam when there is a war in your own country?' he went on.

Why was he angered by my intervention? It could not be because I was black and female and from Africa. I decided to stick to his question and responded at the face value. 'I am a Christian, and this is a Christian country. The war in Vietnam is for me a counter witness to the Gospel of Christ. When Muslims in Nigeria say to me, see what this Christian country is doing, I have no response. As far as I am concerned, wherever people who call themselves Christians work against life, refrain from seeking justice and peace, a prophetic word is called for, and I say it here as I'll say it in Nigeria – seek peace and pursue it with justice. I am here today because the Church is one. What the Church in

Florida does affects the image of the Church in Nigeria.' My interlocutor may not have been satisfied, but he did not ask any more questions., Neither did he walk out on me. Since the Uppsala Assembly 1968 I have seen the ecumenical movement struggle against poverty, sexism and racism, inspired by the good news of the Bible.

The experience of participation

Participating in the ecumenical movement, from small workshops and large conferences to addressing one convention of 10,000 people, has been exciting and awe-inspiring. God is doing something bold and fresh through this movement in which we dare to live in the future. In the youth world, I joined in declaring that youth is in God's world. Young people belong to today's structures, and their thinking and hopes ought to be part of what counts for deciding the moves of the communities to which they belong.

The actual travelling has taken me to most parts of the world, even beyond the Arctic Circle. In the world's metro- and megapolis there have been ecumenical encounters, and I have made myself at home in villages and in five-star hotels. I have been stripped naked by vigilant customs officers while at other times I have been met and ushered into VIP lounges. Between these extremes is the usual scrutiny of my passport and luggage at most airports, while my companion ecumenical travellers go through unstopped. Travelling to these ecumenical encounters I have undergone the challenge and humiliation that comes with being black, woman and African.

Yet in all this I have come to appreciate the preoccupations of many nations and the attitudes of many persons. I have experienced care, solidarity and friendship, even sisterhood. Above all I have come face to face with what it means to belong to the worldwide reality of the Church of Jesus Christ. I have joined in promoting young people, in struggling against racism, sexism, economic domination and poverty. I joined in witnessing to the love and care of

140

God and in struggling to clarify the Church's mission and the meaning of the Gospel for today. I have seen the Student Christian Movement reshape itself to cater to the phenomenon of worker-students, and the WCC give increased attention to women and the emphases identified by women. I have seen the WCC grow from a northern organisation with a mission to the south to a global organisation that sings, prays and reads the Bible in a multitude of languages, and has in its leadership young people, women, clergy and lay persons from the south and from the north, people of all ethnic origins. I have felt myself a daughter of God among other children of God.

What has been inspiring

Participating in theological and Biblical reflections in connection with worship and Bible study and discussions of human challenges has been the particular way in which I have shared in the ecumenical movement and grown up spiritually and theologically. Among the theological motifs that have stayed with me are the WCC Assembly theme of 'Behold I make all things new', the studies of the unity of humanity that have raised the issues of gender, race and class in the context of ecclesial unity. I have returned very often to the challenges of participation in the church, what Christians understand the church to be, and how we contribute one and all to the building up of the Church for witness in the world. Over and above all this is the inspiration of common worship.

PRAYER

When we, one and all, can empty ourselves
of all that divides and come to God,
when one and all we seek to be clothed
in the unity that is a gift of God,
Jesus, sustain us and bring us
in the unity of the Triune God.

Sentences for discussion

The prophetic word
Whenever people who call themselves Christians work against life, refrain from seeking justice and peace, a prophetic word is called for ... I am here ... because the Church is one. What the church in Florida does affects the image of the Church in Nigeria.

Seizing opportunities
My ecumenical journey has not been an interior one. It has been a matter of participating in the movement as opportunties presented themselves.

Ofelia Ortega

Executive Director, Programme on Theological Education of the
World Council of Churches for Latin America and the Caribbean.
Presbyterian-Reformed.

> *Listen! I am standing at the door, knocking; if you
> hear my voice and OPEN THE DOOR, I will come
> in to you and eat with you, and you with me.*

Revelation 3.20

Ecumenical encounter with local congregations

I was born in a traditional Catholic poor home. I was bap-
tized at an early age. I was the daughter of a mother committed to giving religious instruction to her children. It
seemed natural to go to the nearby church, a Baptist congregation that was rendering many social services to the
community.

The pastor was a lay medical doctor with a medical lab-
oratory beside the church building; he had a great sense of
humour and received in a joyful atmosphere a great number of children and young people. The poor were very
much part of Dr Martinez' congregation.

When I was four years old I moved to the Presbyterian
Church. This was due to the fact that the Presbyterian
school La Progresiva was offering opportunity for poor
women to pay the school fees of their children by washing
the clothes of the boarding students.

Now, when I look back, I realise that these two institutions were exercising a *diakonia* ministry in my home town
of Cárdenas, Cuba. Thus, faith and social commitment were
very much part of my early ecumenical encounters.

Ecumenical encounter with my own contextual
reality

Nevertheless, it was only in the sixties, after the triumph of
the Cuban Revolution, that I found myself going beyond
the church's walls to work in the Illiterate Campaign (1961)

organised by the Cuban government, churches and non-governmental organizations in Cuba. During this time the youth and young adults of the local congregations went to the slum areas in Cárdenas to a place called 'La Arrocera'. There we built a multiple-use building that served as a place for liturgy and for teaching illiterate people. It functioned at the same time as a community building where the poor people could meet and plan how to organize their lives together. It was a wonderfully participatory and democratic process, and women were the main protagonists. This 'ecumenical encounter' helped me to recognize that to be truly ecumenically-minded you need to 'break out of the circle of self-absorption and pay heed to the bloodied faces of our fellow human beings for they are the great sacrament of God, the signs and instruments of authentic divine reality. If we do not share life with the oppressed, then we do not share life with God'.[1]

It is true that 'the Christian life, while intensively personal, is always communal, the privatisation of piety is not part of the Christian tradition and it undermines the Christian life ... Christian spirituality is therefore the spirituality of Christian community. But it is not Christian community lived in isolation from the world'.[2]

Encounter with a passionate teacher

I met him in Cuba in the early sixties. He was of small size, simple, calm, quiet, a reflective Asian type of person. His name was C. I. Itty. He was a member of the Syrian Orthodox Church and a citizen of India. How could he influence my life? Is it possible that an Orthodox lay theologian from India could influence and shape the ecumenical commitment of a Presbyterian woman pastor from Cuba? I will have to answer in the affirmative: Yes! And this is precisely the miracle or miracles that happen every day in our ecumenical circles; this is what we call the 'ecumenical virus'; this is what it is to be 'infected' by it.

He visited us in Cuba when he was working with the laity programme of the World Council of Churches. He

committed himself to the teaching of the poor by working
in India and Indonesia as a teacher with the Student Christian Movement in the fifties, and continued with the World
Council of Churches' Youth sub-unit (1960–63); then laity
(1963–70); and later the newly-created Development Department of the World Council of Churches – CCPD (1970–79),
and finally as a consultant to the Youth Department of the
United Nations Economic and Social Commitment for Asia
and the pacific (UN-ESCAP) in Bangkok.

C. I. Itty always gave human relations priority over any
structural or institutional obligations. For this reason when
he saw me in the middle of the crowd that surrounded him
at the encounter organized by the Ecumenical Council of
Cuba with people from different confessions, he approached me with a soft voice and asked me: 'What are the
future plans for your life?' I was surprised by this direct
question. I was preparing myself to go to Great Britain to
do a Masters degree Course on Christian Education. I
shared my plans with him. He moved his head as people
from India do and told me: 'You must go to Bossey
Ecumenical Institute in Geneva, Switzerland ... you need to
receive more ecumenical insights to help the ecumenical
movement in Cuba.' I was not convinced by his comment.
Why did I need to be more involved in the ecumenical
movement? Why did I need to learn more about it? What
was the ecumenical movement about?

Then we went together to the summer camp of the
Presbyterian church for a pastors' retreat — and there in the
chapel (it was an open chapel without walls, in the middle
of the Cuban countryside with a beautiful view of the peasants' homes called 'bohios', surrounded by palm trees) he
gave a presentation where he asked us to look at the fields
and at the peasants working near by and told us: 'The
Church needs to be like this chapel, open doors seeing
always what surrounds it, without losing the perspective of
those who work and live near us. A church without walls!
An open church! This is what ecumenism is all about'.

C. I. Itty's understanding of the ecumenical movement

came from his own experience: what he calls 'signs of conversion'.[3]

A new conversion to the world, a new involvement in the affairs of our society and its demand for social change.

A conversion to mission, to confront the non-Christians with the message of the Gospel.

A new rhythm of life, worship and work, contemplation and activity, detachment and involvement, social services and social action, suffering and joy, doubt and hope, repentance and forgiveness.

New understanding of the cosmic view of redemption, Christian universalism, the priestly character of the Church and a sacramental view of life and work.

After this encounter with C. I. Itty I was totally convinced and in 1967 my church sent me to the Ecumenical Institute in Bossey. This radically changed my life and the direction of my ministry in Cuba. I participated in the Graduate School (October 1967 — February 1968) and spent three months after this experience visiting lay academies in Europe in the first CCLT programme of the WCC (lay training course for lay Christian leaders – eighteen people from different parts of the world) and as a culmination of this learning experience my church sent me as a delegate to the WCC Assembly in Uppsala, Sweden.

My understanding and practice of ecumenism had enlarged so much that, since I was in Bossey, I thought it impossible to live an ecumenical experience without visiting the Vatican. So I organized a study trip with my room-mate during the Christmas break. We were received by Father Thomas Stransky and the Pontifical Council for Christian Unity in a formal way, and this experience of two Bossey students led the way to the inclusion afterwards of an officially invited visit of the Bossey students to the Vatican during every Graduate School programme.

I returned to Cuba with a 'life commitment' to the ecumenical movement. On my arrival I was named Director of the Study Center of the Ecumenical Council of Cuba (1969) and I worked with the churches that belong to the Council in a Sunday school Ecumenical Curriculum that the churches in Cuba used for over ten years. C. I. Itty's 'Open Church' and 'The Church without Walls' is still a permanent call and a living reality for me.[4]

PRAYER

Loving God, we confess that we have fallen short of your will that we live in unity. We claim to be members of the unbroken Body of Christ, yet we have gone our separate ways. We use our limited experience in knowing Christ to judge and exclude others. We come to you in worship, yet we have not been reconciled with those we have offended. O God, we who belong to your Church have lost touch with people outside its fold. We are busy keeping ourselves pure and refuse to reach out to others in love.

We pray you...open our hears, so that we may feel the breath and play of your Spirit.

Unclench our hands, so that we may reach out to one another and touch and be healed. Open our lips that we may drink in the delight and wonder of life.

Unclog our ears to hear your agony in our inhumanity. Open our eyes, so that we may see Christ in friend and stranger.

Breathe your spirit into us, and touch our lives with the life in Christ.

Help us to build up open communities of faith and struggle.

Amen.

Sentences for discussion

The ecumenical virus
This is what we call the 'ecumenical virus'; this is what it is to be 'infected' by it.

The human factor

C. I. Itty always gave human relations priority over any structural or institutional obligations. For this reason when he saw me in the middle of the crowd that surrounded him at the encounter organized by the Ecumenical Council of Cuba with people from different confessions, he approached me with a soft voice and asked me: 'What are the future plans for your life?'

Open doors

'The Church needs to be like this chapel, open doors seeing always what surrounds it, without losing the perspective of those who work and live near us. A church without walls! An open church! This is what ecumenism is all about.'

NOTES

1. Leonardo Boff, *Way of the Cross – Way of Justice* (Maryknoll, 1982), pp. 47-8.

2. John S. de Gruchy, *Cry Justice: Prayers, Meditations and Readings from South Africa* (Maryknoll, 1984), p. 25.

3. See C. I. Itty's biography in *Catalizing Hope for Justive: a tribute to C. I. Itty*, edited by Wolfgang R. Schmidt, World Council of Churches (Geneva, 1987), p. xi of the introduction by Wolfgang R. Schmidt

4. The metaphor that Dr Letty M. Russel used in her book *Church in the Round: Feminist Interpretation of the Church* (Westminster, 1993), helps us to understand the concept of 'Open Church' or 'Church in the Round' better.

John S. Pobee

Co-ordinator of Ecumenical Theological Education of Unit I on Unity and Renewal, World Council of Churches. Member of the Second Anglican-Roman Catholic International Commission. *Anglican.*

No institutional entry point

In ecumenical circles most stories of ecumenical involvement begin with membership of ecumenical institutions such as the World Student Christian Federation, the Student Christian Movement, the YMCA, the YWCA, the Ecumenical Institute at Bossey. I had no such luck or experience. My contact begins with persons who were engaged in one way or other with the work of the World Council of Churches.

Personalities make ecumenism real

As an undergraduate at the University of Ghana, I sat at the feet of Christian G. Baeta for the Old Testament and West African Religions. Originally a Presbyterian, he had in the 1930s participated in the famous Tambaram (Madras) Conference of the International Missionary Council. By the time I was his student, he was serving on the Central Committee of the WCC and on the Commission of the erstwhile Theological Education Fund. Every so often he was away from the country on some assignment or other. Snippets of his 'globetrotting' percolated down to us through his lectures but not in systematic exposés. But through this person my consciousness of the WCC was dimly raised. Years later I pulled his leg by asking him: 'Why are you always travelling?' He quietly looked at me and told me a parable: 'John, the piglets asked their mother: "Why do you have a big mouth?" The mother replied: "Wait till you grow old and ask me this question".' There was no exegesis of it, but the message was clear. Years later, every time I was to travel, he also came to ask: 'So, John you also are going?' His was the prophetic voice in respect of my later involvement in ecumenical life!

In 1972 when I was senior lecturer in the Department for the Study of Religions, University of Ghana, we were visited by the Revd Desmond Tutu, then assistant director of the Theological Education Fund. It fell to my lot to show him round the University and Trinity College (the interdenominational seminary). At the end of the visit he mentioned his intention to invite me to the summer meeting of the Commission of TEF in Bromley. And so it is that in July 1973 I participated in my first TEF meeting. That, with hindsight, was my launching into formal ecumenism.

At the meeting of the Commission one was struck by the dialogue between persons of different races, denominations and circumstances around a theme, a sensitive one at that. The meeting gave me a glimpse of what ecumenical life could be like. Two persons in particular represented to me what I was to learn to be essential equipment for ecumenism: Aharon Sapsezian who was the Assistant-Director for Latin America and Desmond Tutu. They represented in varying mix the combination of incisive mind, zeal and humour. That has remained with me in my ecumenical pilgrimage till today. In my ecumenical involvement I have carried intellectual rigour, zeal and humour as my equipment.

I also learnt that ecumenism is encounter, nay engagement of people, in their particularity, and their oneness in humanity. It helped me to understand in a deeper way Bonhoeffer's statement that 'to be a Christian does not mean to be religious in a particular way, to make something of oneself (a sinner, a penitent or a saint) on the basis of some method or other, but to be a man'.[1] Since then my task in the ecumenical pilgrimage is to search for a new anthropology that will make it possible to affirm that 'the earth is the Lord's and all that is in it.' (Psalm 24.1). I was to learn later that the WCC had the *humanum* studies, and it is for me a matter of regret and concern that that has not been continued.

JOHN S. POBEE

A Department for the Study of Religions points to ecumenism

My undergraduate work was done in the Department of Divinity of the University College of Ghana, then in special relationship with the University of London. Of that department, the presuppositions and programme as reflecting the assumption of British tertiary education and theory, I have written in the context of the programme on Theological Education Consultation on Ministerial Formation.[2] But already when I was *in statu pupillari*, the nationalist government was challenging the department to go beyond Christian theology to recognize the religious pluralism of the nation, and take into consideration the consequence of that reality for the way theology is done. Its challenge was a catalyst in the evolution of that department of divinity into a 'Department for the Study of Religions'. That creation sought to introduce students to the scientific and comprehensive study of the entire religious aspect of human life, with all its personal, social and philosophical involvements.[3] But in addition it sought to promote engagement with indigenous African religions. At that point these were pooh-poohed as superstitious. Above all, it sought to foster encounter between the persons behind the religious labels.

For many the prospect of metamorphosis from Department of Divinity to Department for the Study of Religions was a cause of apprehension, especially for two reasons: fear of lowering of standards and fear of the demotion of Christianity. However, I have been persuaded by my involvement in it that to recognize religious pluralism and secularism, was to be taught that God urges on us the lesson of responsible freedom. Each one, speaking for his own tradition, must say his piece, elucidating his understanding of our co-existence.'[4]

Pluralism – a challenge to ecumenical vision

My working life, after my studies at Cambridge University, has been largely in the Department for the Study of Religions, at the University of Ghana. That has determined to a

151

large extent my ecumenical pilgrimage. For it has taught me that pluralism of cultures, peoples, religions, and ideologies constitutes the context of our pilgrimage of faith and theology. For that reason theology cannot be meaningfully done only within the resources of the Christian heritage. Indeed 'for the vast majority of the poor the language and ideals of their respective religious traditions, their scriptures, myths, folklore are the primary source of inspiration in their struggle for liberation. A theology that does not recognize this fact, and which does not speak to or speak through such peoplehood can end up being an esoteric luxury for a Christian minority.'[5] Thus my awakening to the context of pluralism has been key to my ecumenical pilgrimage.

It has also sharpened my understanding of theology as an academic discipline. Intellectual rigour should be combined with feeling and doing. In other words, theology is not only reflection but also participation in the good news of God. Further, theology must have a missiological orientation. But that missiological orientation is not to be understood as seeking to convert others or being apologetic; it is more like the process of building a 'community of communities' under the inspiration of the rule of God.

The awakening to pluralism has reached the heart of my Christology. It has raised for me the question of what has been variously described as the finality or absoluteness of Christ. But with my sensitivity to the issue of pluralism, I prefer to describe it as the uniqueness of Christ. That for me is the heart of my confession of faith in an ecumenical context, what it means to affirm as a Christian that 'Jesus Christ is the same yesterday, today and forever' (Hebrews 13.8).

Travelling with the WCC

My initial awakening to the context of pluralism through the department for the study of religions was deepened further by my movement in the circles of TEF and its successor bodies. The encounter with Latin America and Asian theologians through TEF etc, certainly enriched my ecumenical consciousness. Conversely, I brought my experiences from the department to that ecumenical arena of discussions. In the *oikoumene* each person is at once a learner and a teacher.

One of the characteristic features of the ecumenical agenda is inclusiveness. That African life is male-dominated hardly needs arguing. I come from a family, however, where both parents did everything to affirm all the children, three boys and three girls. The women had the best possible upbringing and education. As a boy I was always ill and the devotion of my mother to my well-being served to strengthen my respect for women. My involvement in the ecumenical movement increased my sense of the inclusion of women in community of women and men. I now met and engaged and was engaged by some able and fine women, for example Brigalia Bam of South Africa, Leah Tutu of South Africa, Mercy Amba Oduyoye of Ghana, Mrs Mercy Aguta of Nigeria, Elsa Tamez of Costa Rica, Lorine Tevi of Fiji, Barbara Brown Zikmund of USA.

The encounters were not all pleasant. Two examples should suffice. When I had finished editing the book 'New Eyes For Reading' (feminist perspectives in Bible Study), a woman went behind my back to say 'Why should John Pobee, an African male and bachelor, do this? A man with such credentials can only be sexist'. I stood my ground, refusing to be pushed off a track in which I had genuine personal interest. Secondly, I was 'browned-off' by some of the rhetoric of simplistic statements from the USA, appropriating perfectly human traits and qualities for women only, and doing so in ways that do not make for community of women and men. I have learnt in the ecumenical debate one's integrity should be transparent and sometimes a heated exchange may be necessary, without hating the other.

Such experiences motivated me to seek to bring to the surface feminist perspectives from the South, not only to balance some Northern perspectives but also out of the conviction that the voices of one region alone did not constitute an ecumenical perception. Ecumenism demanded that the voice of each should be heard in the dialogue of the peoples of the *oikoumene*. That commitment took the form of my involvement in the organisation and agenda of the Circle of African Women in Theology. My collaboration with several leaders, especially Mercy Oduyoye, Nyambura Njoroge and Musimbi Kanyoro, has been a labour of love and a mutual enrichment.

New understanding of theology

Since January 1984 I have been serving as an executive of the WCC's programme on 'Ecumenical' Theological Education. That was, of course the successor of TEF. So in a real sense, my sojourn in the WCC secretariat continues my earlier work as commissioner of TEF. It has given me new perspectives on theology and theological education:

Theological education should have at once intellectual rigour and missiological vocation. Hence the necessity for all theology to be contextual and address the hopes and fears of people, and not just deal in universals and abstraction. Theology is not just a discipline; it is a life-giving instrument.

Theology is the patrimony of the whole people of God, not only in the sense that it belongs to the stream of tradition of the people of God but also in the sense that each and every one is to give an account of the faith. So in addition to the theological work of the professional theologian, I have learnt to make space for what has been called 'Theology by the People'.

Theology should be informed by the rediscovery of God's preferential option for the poor. This is both a methodological issue and a matter of spirituality which is the dynamo of mission and ecumenism, an expression of the holistic understanding of reality. It means a preference for counter-hegemonic perspective of the oppressed and the marginalized. It is a continuing struggle to make this perspective real in Africa, my home.

The Associations of Theological Institutions in the regions

have been partners of the theological education projects with which I have been involved. Those have proved more ecumenical than some of the ecumenical institutions because in them there is considerable trans-denominational participation and more extra-Christian awareness. I thus learnt to look beyond the formal structures to see the ecumenism.

An Anglican pursuing ecumenism

I am an Anglican. That 'English thing' is troubling for the non-Anglo-Saxon Anglicans. So it has been my life-long and abiding challenge to discover how to be at once African and yet Anglican, to discover what jewel(s) an African Christian and that, an Anglican, brings to adorn the crown of Christ.

I had the opportunity to serve on the Inter-Anglican Theological and Doctrinal Commission whose report was published as *For the Sake of the Kingdom* (Anglican Consultative Council 1986). In that forum of the same and one Anglican Communion I learnt to fight in love for the African jewel alongside other jewels. I learnt to resist firmly without bitterness and in charity what sounded like arrogance or the doctrinaire positions of some colleagues. I was enriched by intense engagement with such individuals as the late Bishop Lakshman Wickremasinghe of Sri Lanka or Bishop Donald Robinson, retired Archbishop of Sidney.

Again, I was one of the Anglican delegation on the Second Anglican-Roman Catholic International Commission. The enrichment that this gave to my life and ecumenical pilgrimage could be a whole book in itself. Let me, however, just signal some of the growth-points. First, I learnt that Anglicans must be an enigma to others and to themselves. The internal debate between High Church Anglicans and Low Church Anglicans must have been baffling to non-Anglicans. And so I have had to face the question: who is this Anglican in dialogue with Rome?

Second, deep friendships developed between the persons across the denominational lines, in spite of the fact that down the years we had demonised one another as denominations. And so I caught something of a vision of ecumenism as recognizing the other as also a member of the one household of God, so as to live in humanity with one another, in spite of differences.

Third – and that is the corollary of the second point – is the experience of pain, especially at our inability to share the Lord's table. I learnt to have great respect and affection for the Roman Catholic Bishop of Savannah, Georgia, USA – Bishop Raymond Lessard. We ate together, had drinks together, prayed and worshipped together and yet we could not bring the friendship to a fulfilment at the Lord's table in spite of a longing to do so. Was that the prompting of the Holy Spirit? That was a recurring, most painful experience. That story raised points for ecumenical pilgrimage:

How far do you take church discipline, and what responsibility do you assume for drawing the lines *vis à vis* church discipline?

Is there room for what I call 'holy disobedience', when in respect I can refuse church discipline? And how does one do so without being a stumbling block to others?

What is truth? This is an old question but very much alive in ecumenical encounters. One thing I have learnt is that truth as seen by humans at any one time is never so final that it cannot be revised. That I believe to be an ecumenical awakening.

Fourth, I have learnt that there is something like the 'politics' of ecumenism. There is a need to be persuasive in dislodging people from positions they have held sometimes from infancy. Some come to discussions with their constituency looking over their shoulders: I do not pooh-pooh that because it reflects a sense of responsibility for others. But we have to ask how far that can be allowed to determine the course of ecumenical debate? I have learnt that real as politics may be in any ecumenical situation, never shall politics in the sense of power-seeking and anxiety to score points, be predominant in ecumenical debate. Politics must be subject to the promotings and guidance of the Holy Spirit which leads into all truth.

Drawing the threads together

Let me attempt to draw the threads together. My ecumenical pilgrimage begins with the persons who mediated the ecumenical vision. But my circumstances as a person from the South and from a pluralistic context faced me with stark questions of ecumenism. At the heart of it is: what is a human being, across the divides of gender, race, tribe, creed, denomination, and so on? In this regard encounters and exchanges of persons from different backgrounds are important. My worry is how to multiply my privileged experience in an age of fractious political realities. My privilege of being involved in some institutional arms of the ecumenical movement has been enriching and it has also raised difficulties. It is a privilege and not a right. It is a privilege with responsibility.

I can be an Anglican and yet ecumenical. Time was when some argued with me that to be ecumenical required of me to give up my denominational involvement. Out of that struggle I came to the conviction that if you know not whence you come, neither do you know whither you go. I am an Anglican, but I live it with a sense of a wider *oikoumene* and with no apology to make. It may be I am helped by the characteristic Anglican emphasis on the *via media*, to stress provisionality in my ecumenical pilgrimage.

My ecumenical awakening and commitment represent the confluence of several things: encounter with personalities, my context of pluralism, the challenge of politicians and involvement in some instruments of ecumenism which deepened my ecumenical sense. Ecumenism I have discovered to be the hermeneutic for making sense of my life in a world of peoples. But I have also learnt that spirituality has to be the dynamo of ecumenism. Institutional ecumenism, especially the WCC, helped me name or named for me the elements of ecumenism about me, in personalities, in the reality of the world around me and in the vocation to worship the one, triune Lord in the beauty of holiness.

Out of all this certain phrases have become key to my ecumenical pilgrimage: Excellence defined in terms of quality, authenticity and creativity; involvement and engagement; listening and hearing; being human sharing a common humanity with others, humility and sense of humour. Coming to these phrases which represent indices of my pilgrimage has been an enlightenment and grace, without which the ecumenical pilgrimage will run aground.

PRAYER

O most Holy trinity
I am one man, but you are Three in One
I am an individual, but you are Community
I am one person, you are Communion
May my encounter with you renew me
As your encounter with the two on the Emmaus
*   road renewed them*
May my heart burn within me, as you speak to me
*   too in diverse ways*
Help me to know that you come to me, as of old, by
The Galilean lakeside, as one without a name
So that I may be responsible to you in others
In your whole creation and Lord, take the
Fragments that we enjoy of your Bounty at our
Tables and multiply them to fill the less
Fortunate of the world.
*   O most Holy Father, make us holy*
*   O most holy Son, make us holy*
*   O most holy Spirit, make us whole.*

Sentences for Discussion

Responsible freedom
Ecumenism can easily degenerate into unprincipled openness ... Time was when some argued with me to give up my denominational involvement. Out of that struggle I came to the conviction that if you know not whence you come neither do you know whither you go.

Diversity
The voices of one region alone did not constitute an ecumenical perception. Ecumenism demanded that the voice of each should be heard in the dialogue of the peoples of the *oikoumene* ...

Pluralism of cultures, peoples, religions and ideologies constitutes the context of our pilgrimage of faith and theology ...

Koinonia
Deep friendships developed between the persons across the denominational lines, in spite of the fact that down the years we had demonised one another as denominations.

Spirituality
Spirituality ... is the dynamo of mission.

NOTES

1. Dietrich Bonhoeffer, *Letters and Papers from Prison* (London: SCM, 1967), p. 118.

2. John S. Pobee, *Ministerial Formation, Department for the Study of Religions, University of Ghana*, in *Ministerial Formation Geneva: Programme on Theological Education* (Geneva, WCC, 1979), pp. 64-67.

3. C. G. Baeta, *The Relationships of Christians with Men of Other Living Faiths* (Legon, Ghana: Ghana Universities Press 1971), p. 3.

4. *Ibid.*, p.9.

5. Paul Rajashekar, *Theological Education in a Pluralistic Context: An Overall Statement: in Ministerial Formation in a Multifaith Milieu. Implications of Interfaith Dialogue for Theological Education*, eds Sam Amirtham and Wesley Ariarajah (Geneva: WCC 1986), p. 108.

Avery D. Post

Former President, United Church of Christ. *United Church of Christ.*

I BELIEVE that the roots of one's ecumenical awareness, both secular and Christian, are very deep and not easily accessible. While, for me, there have been dozens of influential ecumenical encounters over the years in the context of the Church, what seems to have been far more shaping of my awareness was what happened to me in my early years in a particular family, school and community; and in experiences that nurtured a vision of wholeness; as well as others that introduced me to the costs of brokenness.

Our family home was in heterogeneous New England communities. I played and ranged widely and ecumenically in them. But also, with a private bent, I did a good deal of watching, listening, absorbing. I remember being intrigued by the stories from neighborhood families who had recently arrived from eastern and southern Europe. The children in those families were among my first friends, and I loved being in their homes. In some cases they represented a welcome world of difference.

I have to reach far back and way down to capture my early discovery of otherness – to use one of the 'in' words in contemporary theology – and the enjoyment of difference in the midst of wholeness. It was from those early encounters that I developed and have kept a critical perspective on provincialism, where I found myself energized by living openly, ranging far, sitting loose, and sometimes breaking loose. In terms of early faith history, I cannot imagine that I perceived anything but a very big, ecumenical God.

Nothing, however, was more shaping of my awareness than what occurred in the crucible of a painful divorce that split my family. It was in and through that experience that I identified existentially with all brokenness, including the broken family of humankind, as well as with all wished-for healing and wholeness, what I would later call the vision of a reconciled and reconciling unity.

It was from such beginnings that I joined a church, went to college, during World War II served in the U.S. Navy, and began to ponder a life work. I measured the life of the local church with the criterion of width or breadth. College awakened me to the boundless resources of world literature. Navy life was radically pluralistic. Now, as I reflect, it does not surprise me that my first career goals were in public service and what I then called 'politics'.

From this 'proto-ecumenism' the rest unfolded: during my 'teen' years and early twenties. A great deal of Bible reading set off ecumenical signals; the simple awareness that Jesus was an ecumenical person; a lifework decision for an ordained ministry that would be astride Church and world; theological studies in an ecumenical seminary with faculty and friends associated with the Student Christian Movement and the birthing of the World Council of Churches; then the serious weighing of a missionary career in Asia; early inclinations to worry about the Church and churches as closed systems rather than communities of freed and free people living openly, responsively, caringly in the whole world. I can still remember the racing excitement that I felt when I truly heard the prayer of Jesus for unity: 'I in you ... you in me ... they in us' in John 17, and how right it was to begin reciting the first syllables of a theology of one body and one blood.

Who were the mentors, and what were the mentoring influences from then on? The list is long and will never be complete. A literature teacher in college, several poets, a few novelists, many elected public leaders who were also global citizens. In seminary, Kenneth Scott Latourette, H. Richard Niebuhr and several students active in ecumenical youth conferences mentored my ecumenical awareness. Later, in the Church, there were some wide-spirited colleagues in ministry, and the valued companionship of many associates in national church leadership in my own and other denominations, as well as in the World Council of Churches and in the Christian leadership in other countries of the world, whom I have been privileged to know and with whom I have served. I began to list them by name, and found the list too impossibly long and wide-ranging, so long that the danger of inadvertent exclusion leads me to acknowledge such colleagues as a group. They and I know who they are.

Living and serving as a church pastor during the birthing years of the United Church of Christ, the World Council of Churches, and the National Council of Churches had a profound mentoring influence. I found especially helpful the books that prepared for and reported on the Amsterdam (1948) and Evanston (1954) Assemblies of the World Council of Churches.

Through the years, the ecumenical mind, spirit and vision of my life partner, Peg Post, have been a very great influence.

For me, ecumenical growth came through one encounter after another. I now think of them as bursts – bursting moments after which I would exclaim silently or aloud, "Now there! There it is!" I share just a few of them in cinematic fashion.

... the exquisite sermon preached by His Beatitude Ignatio IV of the Greek Orthodox Patriarchate of Antioch and All the East at a World Council of Churches meeting of Moscow in 1987 on the text 'Speaking the truth in love, we are to grow up in every way into him who is the head, into Christ' (Ephesians 4.15) ...

... those days in the early 1970s when the ecumenical community in Boston struggled to be a ministry for peace and justice during the busing crisis ...

... that United Church of Christ General Synod in 1981 that voted and celebrated an ecumenical partnership with the Evangelical Church of the Union in East and West Germany, the first of others to follow ...

... that 1981 Central Committee Meeting in Dresden when members persevered in the effort to define an equitable and just participation of women in the life of the World Council of Churches ...

... those private meetings of Church leaders from the USSR and eastern Europe with U.S. church leaders in Karlovy-Vary, Czechoslovakia, during the chilling ambiguities of the Cold War era.

About all of the above, one could say, 'Now there! There it is!'

... those many marches in Washington of people from the whole inhabited earth witnessing for civil rights, peace in Vietnam, economic justice and policy changes in Central America ...

... the worship of the worldwide Christian community in the tents at the World Council of Churches Assemblies in Vancouver and Canberra ...

... those Bible studies, led by former World Council of Churches General Secretary Philip Potter in Central Committee meetings, especially the one focussing on the New Testament word 'house' (*oikos*) ...

... that 1985 gathering of ecumenical leaders in Harare, Zimbabwe, to express solidarity with the Christian community in South Africa in its struggle to defeat the system of apartheid, followed by the organization of the US Emergency Committee on Southern Africa ...

... that 1987 Ash Wednesday witness in the Rotunda of the Capitol in Washington when five representative church leaders prayed penitently about the inhumaneness of US policies in Central America ...

These were bursting moments. 'Now there! There it is!'

... that discovery and rediscovery of a sentence in the 1949 Basis of Union of the Congregational Christian Churches and the Evangelical and Reformed Church: 'Believing that denominations exist not for themselves but as parts of the Church, within which each denomination is to live and labor and, if need be, die ...'

For me, that language bursts toward the ecumenical. 'Now there! There it is!'

PRAYER

O God, God alone and alone God, we pray that you will in some way interrupt us, even surprise us with a vision of restored unity in the human family, a way out of brokenness, joy in all the differences from which the bonds of peace are woven, so that whether in worship or on a crowded street we may be overcome with the knowledge and trust that you are one God and we are one people, created and graced to live in this small, fragile neighborhood of the world to which you so graciously came in the person and work of Jesus Christ and are so graciously present in the communion of the Holy Spirit. Amen.

Sentences for discussion

Surprise
For me, ecumenical growth came through one encounter after another. I now think of them as bursts – bursting moments after which I would exclaim silently or aloud, 'Now there! There it is!'

Reconciliation and healing
I identified existentially with all brokenness, including the broken family of humankind, as well as with all wished-for healing and wholeness, what I would later call the vision of a reconciled and reconciling unity.

Local and universal
I developed and have kept a critical perspective on provincialism, where I found myself energized by living openly, ranging far, sitting loose, and sometimes breaking loose.

I measured the life of the local church with the criterion of width or breadth.

Brother Roger of Taizé

Founder and leader of the ecumenical community of Taizé, France. *Reformed.*

SEEING WEEK after week in Taizé, for such a long time now, so many faces of young adults, from Northern and Southern Europe, from Africa, Latin America and Asia, there is always the same astonishment. We were not prepared to welcome so many and we have never had a method. We realize that these young people come with vital questions: How can God be everything for me? What does Christ expect of me? How can I find in Christ a meaning for my life? And we wish to be for them above all men of prayer and listening, never spiritual masters.

With the young adults we welcome, we try to understand that, as he entrusts to us a mystery of hope in an age of shocks and upheavals, Christ enables us to communicate it above all by the lives we live. Words come later, to confirm and support the witness of a life. And in fact, where would we be today if women, men, young people and children too, had not arisen when the human family was doomed to the worst? They did not say, 'Let things take their course!' They prepared a road beyond the oppositions between persons, nations, spiritual families. Their life witnesses to the fact that human beings were not created for hopelessness.

Among those who prepared roads forward in this way, I often return for inspiration to the courage of my own maternal grandmother. During the First World War, her three sons were fighting on the front lines. She was a widow, living north of Paris. Although the bombs were falling all around, she did not want to leave her home so that she could offer a welcome to those who were fleeing – old people, children, pregnant women. She only left at the last minute, when everybody had to flee. From that time on, she was possessed by the deep desire that noone should ever have to go through what she had experienced. She had seen two wars. So she reflected: separated Christians were fighting one another; if only they could be reconciled, since they professed faith in a God of love, and if they could do everything in their power to keep another world war from breaking out! She was from an old Protestant family. To live out within herself a reconciliation without delay, she began to go and pray in a Catholic church.

Was not her intuition that of having discovered a kind of key to the ecumenical vocation ? Did she not enable others to realise that, by reconciling within themselves the stream of faith of their Protestant origins with the Catholic faith, a road forward would open up?

Two things my grandmother did marked me for life: she took risks to help those most afflicted at the time, and she looked for reconciliation within herself. I followed the road she had opened. In 1940, at the beginning of the Second World War while I was still alone in Taizé, I hid refugees whom I had been asked to welcome, people who were running away from danger, Jews in particular. And, to support reconciliations, it became a necessity to create a community of brothers who would live out reconciliation concretely, day after day. That committed us to go to the very end in saying yes for our entire lifetime because of Christ and the Gospel.

I certainly owe to my grandmother the conviction that we shall always have to give an answer to the question: how can we alleviate different forms of human suffering? And until today, this has led my brothers and I to look for ways of sharing the life of the most deprived. Some of us live in poor neighbourhoods in different parts of the world. How could we live in the West unless some of us were sharing the life of the poorest of the poor in the Southern continents? When I see some of my brothers give their lives by living in conditions of great poverty, I say to myself: such a gift of oneself is a burning breath of the Gospel; even from far away it penetrates our whole community.

Our vocation to reconciliation has been supported by many holy witnesses to Christ. Among them, I would like to mention one who, after having lived the United States, became the Patriarch of Constantinople. His name was Athenagoras. In his last years, he was not spared by trials. And yet he remained full of hope. 'In the evening when I return to my room,' he told me one day. 'I leave my worries behind the door and I say: tomorrow!'

I can still see clearly a pilgrimage we made with him by car through the streets of Constantinople. He could not get out of the car himself but each time we passed a spot where a Christian had died for Christ, he asked the driver to slow down or stop. We would say a prayer and then continue on our way.

How can I forget our last visit to Constantinople? As we said goodby, the Patriarch stood in the doorway and, while making the gesture of lifting up the Eucharistic chalice, spoke these final words: 'The cup and the breaking of the bread; there is no other solution remember.'

At the same time, in the middle of the twentieth century, there was a man whose name was John, born in a humble family in the North of Italy. The immense pastoral responsibility entrusted to him undoubtedly brought to full flowering in him exceptional powers of intuition. When he announced a Council, that elderly man, John XXIII, pronounced in 1959 words that are among the most transparent imaginable. They are able to transform and even transfigure that communion of love which is the body of Christ, his Church: 'We will not try to find out who was wrong or who was right, we will only say: let us be reconciled!'

John XXIIII had in him expressions that did away with discouragement. Speaking about 'prophets of doom,' he said publicly one day: 'In the present state of society, these prophets of doom see only ruin and calamity; they say that our age has become much worse, as if everything were perfect in the past; they predict catastrophes, as if the end of the world were near.'

Another of his sayings can have deep relevance today. When he opened the Council, he said, 'Today, the Church prefers to make use of the remedy of mercy rather than to brandish the weapons of severity.'

Our last meeting took place in 1963. Three of us brothers were present. John XXIIII had the deep desire for us not to be worried about the future of our community. The Church is composed of concentric circles, wider and wider, he explained, making circular gestures with his hands. In the situation in which our community found itself, we understood that we could continue along the road on which we found ourselves, without tormenting ourselves with worries that lead nowhere.

PRAYER

O God, we praise you for the multitudes of women, men, young people and children who, throughout the earth, try to be witnesses to peace, trust and reconciliation. In the steps of all the holy witnesses to Christ, from the apostles and Mary down to those of today, enable us day after day to dispose ourselves inwardly to place our trust in the Mystery of the Faith.

Enable us to be among those who, almost without words, show that, for them, God is everything:

those who give their lives in the humble trusting of faith,

those who understand the wounded innocence of a child, of a young person,

those who remain alongside the most deprived,

those who go to the wellsprings of the Gospel in approachimg, by the lives they lead, the holiness of Christ, the Risen Lord.

Sentences for discussion

Surprise
There is always the same astonishment. We were not prepared to welcome so many, and we have never had a method.

Ecumenical apostles

Did she not enable others to realise that, by reconciling within themselves the stream of faith of their Protestant origins with the Catholic faith, a road forward would open up?

Risk

Two things my grandmother did marked me for life: she took risks to help those most afflicted at the time, and she looked for reconciliation within herself.

The common table

As we said goodby, the Patriarch stood in the doorway and, while making the gesture of lifting up the Eucharistic chalice, spoke these final words,' The cup and the breaking of the bread; there is no other solution remember.'

True reconciliation

'We will not try to find out who was wrong or who was right, we will only say: let us be reconciled!' (Pope John XXIII)

William G. Rusch

Director of the Department for Ecumenical Affairs and Assistant to the Bishop, Evangelical Lutheran Church in America, Chicago, USA. *Lutheran.*

WHEN I was recently requested to write a brief vignette which would describe my personal experience in ecumenical formation, I thought initially that this would be a relatively easy task. Actually the invitation caused me to reminisce in some ways that I had not expected. It focussed for me that behind the request is a recognition with which I am in full agreement: for most persons ecumenism is not a natural state; it requires cultivation.

I have a strong conviction based not only on personal experience, but on observation of friends and colleagues around the world, that most persons who are ecumenists never intended to be listed in that particular category of human beings. In other words most individuals who find themselves devoting their time, energy, and talents – to whatever degree they possess them – to the unity of the Church, did not start out that way. Something happened that changed them in fundamental ways.

If ecumenism is an acquired pursuit it is also often a dangerous pursuit. Taken seriously, it does not leave committed women or men as they were before. There is a widening horizon of concern for the greater Church, and often a suspicion on the part of fellow religionists that ecumenists may at times waiver in loyalty to a tribalism because of a fixation on a larger whole – the Church catholic.

If this impression of mine has any validity, it means that most ecumenically committed individuals are products of long processes of development and interaction. Rarely does one experience, one person or one event an ecumenist make!

My life, at least for me, confirms this intuition as I look back on it. Like many persons, I suspect that ecumenical formation was going on when I was not aware of it. The degree to which it is possible for me to trace my ecumenical journey may be too retrospective to allow too many well-founded and general conclusions.

Nevertheless, with that caveat in place, I would identify my educational experience as one of the critical places where I moved from 'being a Lutheran' to 'being a Lutheran with an abiding dedication to the visible unity of Christ's followers'. I learned early in the process that both states of 'being' were not mutually exclusive, but, on the contrary, inseparable. In fact, this insight, I came to understand, is fully compatible with the aspirations of those first 'Lutherans' in the sixteenth century, who accepted that nomenclature with less than total enthusiasm.

Through college, seminary, and graduate school days in this country and in Europe I was fortunate to study with a great variety of teachers, most of whom were deeply committed to the Church, a minority of whom could claim the label 'Lutheran'. They broadened my perceptions of the Church and its history. Friendships and associations of great meaning were established with individuals of common interests and a dedication which transcended national borders.

Such an expansion of view did two things: it made me see my own Christian tradition in the larger perspective, and encounter for myself the deep pain of the separations of Christians – separations explained by the hard decisions of history, but nevertheless a scandal. It gave me greater awareness as to exactly why these divisions are indeed a sacrilege, when they keep brothers and sisters in Christ apart.

Thus surprisingly shaped, I encountered opportunities for ecumenical ministry, which I did not anticipate and which I imagined would be brief chapters in my life. They have grown to represent the greater portion of my life since my ordination. These episodes have usually not been uncomplicated, but they have been immeasurably enriching. Others in the future must, and will, evaluate what has been accomplished. I can only record my deep gratitude in this ministry for the experience of a sense of the greater Church and a host of believers, to which I belong, that is so much more varied, widespread, and numerous than I once could ever have envisaged.

*O God of surprises, who continues to lead your
people in ways beyond our understanding, instil in
us that yearning for the oneness of Christ's followers
in this broken world that we may serve you more
faithfully and reflect to those about us your gift of the
one, holy, catholic, and apostolic Church. This we ask
in Christ's name.*

Sentences for discussion

God's plan
I suspect that ecumenical formation was going on when I was not aware of it.

Openness to change
If ecumenism is an acquired pursuit it is also often a dangerous pursuit. Taken seriously, it does not leave committed women or men as they were before.

Turid Karlsen Seim

Member of the International Roman Catholic-Lutheran Dialogue,
Professor of Theology (New Testament) and Dean of the Faculty
of Theology, University of Oslo, Norway. *Lutheran*

FOR A Norwegian Lutheran of my generation to grow into
ecumenical commitment is almost a conversion. The post-
war Norway of my childhood was a homogeneous society
with the over-all predominant state-church as its religious
face. This face was a rare mix of diverse features: a devoted
Lutheran confessionalism; an almost reformed pietistic
ethos; and rituals maintaining an open folkchurch tradition. When looking back I am struck by the lack of awareness about the presence of other Christian communities in
the country – perhaps apart from Pentecostals, whom we
considered to be members of a revival movement going
wrong, and some Roman Catholic personalities who played
a role in the public debate.

This meant that most discussions about theology and
Christianity happened within a framework of shared presuppositions. Even those who had held the more liberal or
radical position willingly and triumphalistically based their
argumentation on Luther as the norm. The battle was about
the right interpretation of the confessional tradition and
much less about the exclusiveness of this tradition itself. To
some extent any debate was a competition for excellency in
being fully and truly Lutheran. Such was the climate of my
theological upbringing, and it probably impregnated me
with a Lutheran marrow and instincts.

Considering this context, it is indeed peculiar that in my
first real glimpse of personal memory a Roman Catholic sister in her pre-Vatican II habit plays a major role. In my inner
eye I still see the rather scary creature bent over me when
at three years old I came out of the anaesthetic after having
my tonsils removed at the local Roman Catholic hospital.
The experience was traumatic. By no wish of my own I

found myself left in the hands of strangers in a world bereft of everything and everyone close and familiar. But after that I always knew they existed, these strangers in my otherwise self-contained life.

When as a young girl I met the sisters again and lived in one of their houses for a short year, the trauma was replaced by sentiments of attraction. They opened my mind and my heart to a spirituality of communal discipline, of prayers and reflection being carried out, even if I myself did not manage to perform. Worship became an act of the community including and embracing the individual but not depending on my own attempts at the pious works. In a way those Roman Catholic sisters shared with me a spiritual life which, much more than my previous pietistic efforts, represented a life lived by God's grace alone. I did not convert to the Roman Catholic Church; I rather found myself still to be a convinced Lutheran, but both needing and willing to learn from the treasures of other traditions.

Many years later and after my graduation from Divinity School, I spent a year in a Romanian town where the local Lutheran congregation had Hungarian as its language. Since my Hungarian was non-existent, the Sunday service was beyond comprehension and therefore beyond participation. My weekly exercise of singing strange sounds and listening to words I could not understand, made me aware of the fact that Lutheran communication is almost exclusively based on the intelligibility of the spoken word. It is an exercise of the mind, the mouth and the ear.

This is not to question the crucial point that the Gospel should be preached in words which people can understand, in this case: in Hungarian to Hungarians. But for someone who did not share that particular language, there was, apart from what comparative deduction made possible, very little left in which she could truly take part. In contrast to this, the Orthodox liturgy in the same foreign town had the capacity through its visual display and narrative structure to speak to the heart and to the senses beyond any intellectual comprehension. It stirred a theological and intellectual interest as well, but participation was not necessarily dependent on verbal communication and intelligibility.

The fascination of these encounters has lingered with me ever since. The experience was never felt to be a presentation of mutually exclusive options urging a drastic change or choice: conversion to another church was far from my thoughts. Neither did it foster a fastidious personal eclecticism: that to me is a perverted, *à la carte* ecumenism. It rather helped me question the self-sufficiency of my previous quite zealous confessional position and its claim to be complete in itself. It made me aware that what I had believed to be the full picture was a fragment of a mirror long broken. It meant that ecumenical commitment became important beyond any comparative theological endeavor as divine calling to participate in a process of healing – of making whole.

The personal dimension to my ecumenical commitment has been a pilgrimage of spirituality. It has been a quest for spiritual renewal, and it has been shaped through many personal encounters. An important dimension to ecumenism is how friendship is established across borders of prejudice and even animosity. But ecumenism is not to be confused with exotic and exciting travelling. It is more than collecting acquaintances, more than just meeting friends or family all around the world. It has to do with self-recognition. The interrelation between conviction and contextuality more easily recognized in 'the other' than in oneself, has made me aware of my own particular belonging as it also speaks about the accidental circumstance of my own particular place. It is by belonging together that we are made whole.

The professional dimension has been for me the theological questions involved in the strenuous work towards visible unity. Theological reflection is indispensable if we are to remain faithful to the truth and able to discern how the diversity of expressions still conveys the one faith and confirms our common belonging. I firmly and passionately believe that the struggle to make manifest the God-given unity of the church, is a divine imperative serving God's purpose for the whole of creation.

Confront us, O Christ,
with the hidden prejudices and fears
which deny and betray our prayers.
Enable us to see the causes of strife;
remove from us all false sense of superiority.
Teach us to grow in unity with all God's children,
trusting in your mercy now and forever.
Amen

Sentences for discussion

The imperative
I firmly and passionately believe that the struggle to make manifest the God-given unity of the church is a divine imperative serving God's purpose for the whole of creation.

Breaking barriers
An important dimension to ecumenism is how friendship is established across borders of prejudice and even animosity.

The battle was about the right interpretation of the confessional tradition and much less about the exclusiveness of this tradition itself. To some extent any debate was a competition for excellency in being fully and truly Lutheran. Such was the climate of my theological upbringing.

What I had believed to be the full picture, was a fragment of a mirror long broken.

The right place for confessional loyalty
Conversion to another church was far from my thoughts. Neither did it foster a fastidious personal eclecticism: that to me is a perverted, *à la carte* ecumenism. It rather helped

me question the self-sufficiency of my previous quite zealous confessional position and its claim to be complete in itself.

Commitment
Ecumenical commitment became important beyond any comparative theological endeavour as divine calling to participate in a process of healing – of making whole.

Spiritual pilgrimage
The personal dimension to my ecumenical commitment has been a pilgrimage of spirituality. It has been a quest for spiritual renewal.

Doing theology
Theological reflection is indispensable if we are to remain faithful to the truth and able to discern how the diversity of expressions still conveys the one faith and confirms our common belonging.

Krister Stendhal

Bishop of Stockholm, Sweden (retired). *Lutheran.*

I WAS drawn to Jesus and to Church, although my family hardly were active church-goers. Later I got my teenage rebellion by being religious. That was in the Church of Sweden, where over ninety per cent of the population are members, at least formal members of ' the church', as the Swedes say. When people abroad ask Swedes, 'Are you Lutheran?' the answer is either,'I guess so', or, 'No, we are Swedish'.

It is true that the Church of Sweden has given significant leaders to the ecumenical movement from Nathan Söderblom and on, but if the truth be told – our ecumenism was international rather than domestic.

That is also the case for me. I was very active in the high school department of the Student Christian Movement. And that meant our natural ambience was the Student Christian Movement rather than the local church. Our leaders were connected internationally through the World Student Christian Federation. They went to those big meetings and told us about the world of ecumenism.

When I later became involved in some local ecumenism, I can remember myself saying, 'Let's not only be ecumenical to the "right", loving Catholics and Anglicans; we have Jesus in common with the Pentecostals, too'. I was relatively alone in having that urge, yet I think most of us would claim in intellectual honesty that you could not do one thing without the other.

When I finished my doctorate in 1954 I had a choice. I was invited to be director of the Youth Department in the World Council of Churches in Geneva, or I could come to Harvard for two years. We had two children, 4 and 6, and my wife Brita and I decided that this was the time to try Harvard. It turned out to be thirty years. As he often reminded me, Philip Potter became WCC youth director when I said no. I felt I had done my share of youth work ...

When I came to the United States, a totally new world opened up to me. People have perhaps associated me more-with Jewish-Christian relations than with Christian ecumenism. It happened this way. I wrote my dissertation on the Dead Sea Scrolls and the Gospel of Matthew. I had been interested in how to understand the more Jewish-sounding theology of Matthew (compared with John and Luke), and in what was the difference between Paul and Matthew, and so on. I had the feeling that something was wrong with the stereotyped images of the 'Scribes' – what Jesus calls Sages. So I studied Jewish sources. I put the Scrolls into the dissertation, but I certainly had no contact with, nor any conscious interest in, Jews. And that says a lot about my culture and my church. Now of course I am ashamed of this. For me 'the Jews' were the background for the understanding of Jesus, period.

Edwin Wilson had just published a highly popular book on the Scrolls, which *The New Yorker* had run in instalments. Since he was sophisticated about the Scrolls but naïve about the Christian material I was 'on the circuit' a good deal to lecture about the Scrolls and Christianity in both Christian places and synagogues. That was when I met Jews for the first time seriously. That was my entrance into the wider ecumenism.

With that came also the debates at Harvard about whether or not we should have a Center for the Study of World Religions at the Divinity School. The more Barthian[1] members of the faculty were against it:' We shouldn't pollute Christianity and certainly people who were not Protestant Christians should not have the right to vote on appointments ...' etc. I was one of the proponents because I thought it was important. And through that center, especially through the work of Wilfred Cantwell Smith, I became deeply touched by the reality of God's whole menagerie within which not only Judaism but also Christianity is a minority. As I like to say, ' In the eyes of God we are all minorities'. I began to seek a Christian theology of religion. How can I sing my song to Jesus with abandon without feeling that I have to speak badly about others ? I think that is an important question, one which became important also in the World Council of Churches and its dialogue with people of other faiths.

Of course I have over the years also been involved privately and officially in Christian ecumenism. But I have come to feel that it is less and less interesting theologically – the problem being too often institutional rather than spiritual. Full mutual recognition should not be that difficult. Thus I have turned my thoughts more and more to the 'wider ecumenism'. After all *oikumene* means 'the inhabited world', and to limit the word to Christian unity work is already a sign of something being wrong.

Even so, when I served as Bishop of Stockholm from 1984 to my retirement in 1988, it was my duty – which I accepted gladly – to chair the Executive Committee of the Swedish Ecumenical Council. So I was at the center of the domestic and local Swedish ecumenism with Catholics and the Church of Sweden and practically all the 'free churches', the Pentecostals being most reluctant. There were also the Orthodox churches which have come to Sweden through the great array of immigration after the Second World War.

Within the work of theology, I have come to see myself as belonging to 'the department of public health'. How to see to it that we avoid undesirable side-effects of our joyous medicine? The evangelicals are in surgery and the mainline churches are in internal medicine, but there has to be someone in the public health department. And much of that has to do with ecumenism and I think the rules of the game are the same in ecumenical and interfaith dialogue. For the ground-rules must be: 1) Let the others define themselves and 2) Compare equal to equal. We so often compare the ideal of our own with the actual of the other. And 3) We must learn 'holy envy', i.e., to find something beautiful in the other although it is not ours.

PRAYER

O Holy Spirit, giver of many and diverse gifts;
O Holy Spirit who enlivens our imagination
    Let us seek unity in diversity; let us find diversity
in unity – lest our unity be oppressive and our
diversity divisive.
    O Holy Spirit, grant us that most precious gift of
yours by which we can discern what is important.

Sentences for discussion

God's menagerie
And through that center, especially through the work of
Wilfred Cantwell Smith, I became deeply touched by the
reality of God's whole menagerie within which not only
Judaism but also Christianity is a minority. As I like to say,
'In the eyes of God we are all minorities'. I began to seek a
Christian theology of religion. How can I sing my song to
Jesus with abandon without feeling that I have to speak
badly about others?

The real and the beautiful
We must learn 'holy envy', i.e., to find something beautiful
in the other although it is not ours.

NOTES
1. The reference is to Karl Barth.

Emmanuel Sullivan, SA

Franciscan Friar of the Atonement, Episcopal Vicar for Ecumenical Affairs, Diocese of Arundel and Brighton and member of the Committee for Christian Unity of the Catholic Bishops' Conference of England and Wales. *Roman Catholic.*

MY ECUMENICAL pilgrimage had three stages. The first may be traced in what I learned and experienced with my Ulster Protestant mother. The second would be my vocation to become a Franciscan Friar of the Atonement. The third would cover that all-important event in the life of my church – the Second Vatican Council.

My mother came from an Ulster family noted for its sense of tolerance and charity, a deep sense that love enables us to understand in some measure where the other person is 'coming from'. Her mother had fed the poor and homeless as they crossed the family farmland. Her father had been spat upon in Belfast because he had been mistakenly taken for a Roman Catholic. My mother taught my brother and sisters a deep sense of tolerance with charity, qualities she had to exercise, not without difficulty, when she married into a rather narrow Roman Catholic family with Cork[1] connections. But she also had a profound sense of faithfulness to whatever she promised. She had promised, as was the rule in those days, to raise her children as Roman Catholics. She kept that promise above and beyond what one might have expected. She rehearsed us in our catechism lessons and reminded us of our church obligations. She prepared us without much help from my father for life in the Roman Catholic Church.

She did much more than that for me. As the youngest I well remember her little commentaries on the packaged answers of the catechism. She gave me a sense of the greatness of the mystery of God and sense of the love of God expressed in the life and death of Jesus. The grandeur of God and the greatness of God far exceed the limitations and expectations we impose on God in our hearts and minds – and in our churches. This sense of mystery and love of God combined with her inherited sense of tolerance and love of others to open my own mind and heart at a very early age.

The second stage of my ecumenical journey began when I entered prep school at Graymoor with the intention of joining the Graymoor Friars, as they were popularly known. Prior to this I had attended public school in our little village. I had no real experience of formal Roman Catholic education, even less experience of women and men religious. Here was a community founded as an Anglican community in 1898, which had moved into the Roman Catholic Church in 1909. The Society of the Atonement was young and vibrant and filled with promise in 1943. To enter the SA community was to live within the vision and prayer of our Lord as recorded in John 17: 'that all may be one – that the world might believe'. When this community was received into full communion with Rome, its independent life in the Roman Catholic Church was assured because it clearly intended to continue its work for Christian unity and the mission to non-Christians. Those who aspired to join were expected to form their Christian religious life in accord with the Gospel ideal of reconciling Christians in order to help the Gospel of our Lord speak with its true voice in the world.

I remember how much energy and involvement, even when we were young prep students, went into planning and promoting the Week of Prayer for Christian Unity. In those days we called it the Church Unity Octave. The Friars and Sisters of the Atonement had begun this intense period of prayer while yet Anglicans in 1908. They were determined that it would receive a very high place in the life of the Roman Catholic Church. All this was my second inheritance – a vision of and passion for unity. Yet all we could do as Roman Catholics in those days was to keep the ideal of Christian unity alive in the Church and pray for it with spiritual energy. It was hard for Roman Catholics to know how to work for the unity they prayed for. Practically speaking they could understand it only in terms of a return to the Catholic Church on its terms of self-understanding. And then Vatican II was upon us, and the third stage of my ecumenical pilgrimage began.

Vatican II, with its commitment to the ecumenical movement was a moment of grace for Catholics, not least myself. I had experienced tremendous intellectual conflict in the theology I had studied. Theologically speaking, there was no room in it to relate to other Christians as committed members of other churches or communities of faith. Vatican II changed all that – and me. By 1967 I was free to work for Christian unity, to implement the vision and prayer of our Lord in John 17. I could now present a theology of my church as having a real though partial and imperfect communion with other churches. I could now *work* as well as pray for Christian unity. I could put the vision of a renewed Church before others and hold it with profound integrity in my own mind and heart.

I have been fully engaged in the ecumenical movement for twenty-six years. Twenty of these years have been spent in Britain where so many religious divisions have begun. So much of our Christian past is here. The new age of reconciliation and the healing of memories have been my ministry here.

We are shaped by the ministries we engage in. The past twenty-six years have completed my ecumenical formation. I often remind people that my ecumenical commitment enables me to see my life and ministry as one whole thing. I do not commute between the internal life of my church and the life of other churches. Here in Britain we have scrapped the British Council of Churches in favour of another concept – Churches Together. This is a concept developed from a notion John Paul II put in our heads when he visited Britain in 1982. It is simple as a concept and an image for the whole ecumenical movement. It is this. As we work by stages and converge ever so gradually into that unity our Lord willed and prayed for, we look upon ourselves and our churches as pilgrims walking hand in hand. This is the spiritual dynamism that has given the churches of the United Kingdom new hope and energy for the task ahead. It is also part of my ecumenical formation and growth. My personal life and ministry has become fully identified with the whole life of my church which shares in the life of other churches and Christians. This is the commitment and present life of my church. It is mine as well. Ecumenism is a way of life that has pervaded my life.

Let me conclude by saying that the tolerant love I learned from my mother, the sense of mystery and the grandeur of God she imparted, prepared me to receive what my church has given to me through its own response to the inspiration of the Holy Spirit at the time of Vatican II. But there is little doubt in my mind that these gifts have been nourished and developed because the grace of God led me to Graymoor and the Franciscan Friars of the Atonement.

PRAYER

Guide us, O Lord, by your Word and Holy Spirit,
that in your light we may see light,
in your truth find freedom,
and in your will discover peace;
through Jesus Christ our Lord. Amen.

Sentences for discussion

Ecumenical ministry
We are shaped by the ministries we engage in. Ecumenism is a way of life that has pervaded my life.

The other person
Love enables us to understand in some measure where the other person is coming from.

Unity of life
I often remind people that my ecumenical commitment enables me to see my life and ministry as one whole thing.

I do not commute between the internal life of my church and the life of other churches.

NOTES

1. Cork is in the far south-west of the Republic of Ireland.

Mary Tanner

Moderator of the Faith and Order Commission, World Council of
Churches, General Secretary of the Council for Christian Unity,
of the General Synod of the Church of England. *Anglican.*

IT IS IMPOSSIBLE to choose one experience from the kalei-
doscope of ecumenical experiences that have been part of
my life for more than twenty years and which have
strengthened my commitment to the unity of the Church.
There are treasured friendships formed across the boundaries of ecclesial divisions; memories of worshipping with
local congregations – in a Harijan village in India, in a sub-
urb of East Berlin immediately after the fall of the Wall and
in Soweto shortly before the first free elections. There have
been the inescapable moments of struggling with the pain
of being unable to share in the eucharist. There was the time
when an Indian Jesuit friend sat holding my hand as the
Roman Catholic congregation received bread and wine. He
taught me the lesson that we have to bear each other's pain
– even enter that pain on the way to greater unity.

From all of this one 'moment of disclosure' stands out. It
was in January 1992 in Lima, Peru. One hundred and
twenty or so theologians from many different churches
were staying together in a retreat centre on the outskirts of
the town. In that barren country, where it hardly ever rains,
we were enclosed in a beautiful oasis. A stream ran through
the centre of the campus; trees and plants blossomed
around us. For many years the group had worked patiently
to formulate a text setting out all that could be said together
about baptism, eucharist and ministry. The moment came
when the text was finished. We were asked is this text
'mature enough' to go to the churches? The question received unanimous assent. In the silence that followed the
group stood to give thanks for what was on any reckoning
a significant step on the road to unity.

Looking out of the window in that time of silence I saw

we were enclosed in our oasis by a high barbed-wire covered wall. Outside the barren hills rose on every side. Where the scrubby plants gave way to desert were a few small shacks, mostly half-built, where the poor, the unimaginably poor, eked out some sort of living. The Church was there in its comfortable oasis safeguarding its life-giving traditions of baptism, eucharist and ministry while outside was a world of poverty, starvation and death. Unless what we were doing had something – no, everything – to do with that world, we should give up on the seemingly endless round of theological talk. The unity of the Church is not an end in itself: not some comfortable holy huddle separated off from the pain and divisiveness of the world around. The Church is to be a witness to the possibility of healing and unity for all people. The Church is to be 'the world ahead of itself' pointing the way by its own life, preparing the way by its own serving. The unity of the Church and the renewal of the human community belong together ...

PRAYER

O God, holy and eternal Trinity
we pray for your Church in all the world.
Sanctify its life; renew its worship;
empower its witness; heal its divisions;
make visible its unity.

Lead us, with all our brothers and sisters,
towards communion in faith, life and witness
so that, united in one body by the one Spirit,
we may together witness to te perfect unity of your love.
Amen.

The Santiago Prayer, World Council of Churches, 1993

Sentence for discussion

Unless what we were doing had something – no, everything – to do with that world, we should give up on the seemingly endless round of theological talk ... The unity of the Church and the renewal of the human community belong together.

David W. A. Taylor

Former General Secretary of the Consultation on Church Union, Princeton, New Jersey, USA. *Presbyterian.*

IN THE SUMMER of 1961, *Time* magazine printed a cover-story, about a dramatic proposal by Dr Eugene C. Blake to unite churches of this land [the USA] across their traditional lines, both catholic and reformed. Several denominations, it seemed, were taking the proposal seriously and were already beginning to appoint representatives to meet in ecumenical conversation in order to draw up such a plan. What they would be seeking, the article went on to say, was a multilateral church union of a kind that would be simultaneously catholic, evangelical, and reformed. Today's readers will recognize that what was then being reported by *Time* was the birth of what later came to be known as the 'Consultation on Church Union' – or COCU.

For reasons not quite clear to me at the time, I found the story to be immensely exciting. I was a young pastor, and could scarcely wait to share with my colleagues in the local ministerial association my enthusiasm for the story I had read. Much to my surprise, however, several of the ministers present found little to celebrate in this news. Indeed, some were rather critical of it, and a few were downright hostile to the whole idea – though some warmed to the news.

Why should Christian ministers respond so differently to such a straightforward ecumenical initiative? I found that to be quite puzzling at the time, and have often wondered about it since. For me it is a question of the sources of ecumenical caring. What was it that prompted me then, and does so still, to respond affirmatively and with instinctive enthusiasm to the call for Church unity?

To the extent that I know my own mind and heart, I have been able to identify three elements that were, I think, crucial in causing me to respond as I did to the ecumenical

190

vision reported in the 1961 article in *Time* magazine.

In my experience, the first element is surely the traditioning I received in childhood and youth. Curiously, as I recall it, there was little if anything that was specifically 'ecumenical' about it. Indeed, it was Presbyterian to the core; Southern Presbyterian at that – a particularly conservative expression of the genre. And it was intense: rooted in family prayers and Bible reading, memorization of the *Westminster Shorter Catechism*, memorization of vast portions of Scripture and of the hymns of the church, family attendance at Sunday worship both morning and evening, and much discussion at table of the affairs of the church both locally and denominationally.

It might appear that the nurture just described would be calculated to produce the very opposite of ecumenical concern. That has indeed been the case for some of my kin. Nonetheless I give first place to ecclesiastical traditioning as a decisive element in my ecumenical formation. I do so for three reasons.

First, ecumenical formation in my view is a subcategory of spiritual formation. It has little to do with ecclesiastical joinery, but with obedience to Christ's will for the Church.

Second, a thorough traditioning in the doctrine and discipline of any of the mainline Christian denominations will include some attention to the history, doctrine, worship, and polity of the Church – that is to say, 'ecclesiology'. In my view, there is no such thing as an ecumenist who does not care deeply about these things. That is what most distinguishes ecumenical Christianity from individualistic, subjectivistic forms of popular religiosity.

Third, I have never met an identifiable ecumenist who was not also and at the same time a deeply committed participant in his or her own particular church tradition. It is my experience that ecumenical concern tends to strengthen rather than weaken one's understanding, appreciation and attachment to one's own ecclesiastical heritage, at the same time that it deepens one's understanding and appreciation of the traditions of others.

The second discernible element in my own ecumenical formation, after ecclesiastical traditioning, has been the opportunity to participate in ecumenical experiences. This first occurred for me during my freshman year at the university, when I was privileged to attend a conference of the Student Volunteer Movement held at Wooster, Ohio in December, 1943. The impact of such an event is greater than the content of the speeches, all soon forgotten. What such an event does is open up for the participant a wider vision of the holy catholic Church – which is the essence of the ecumenical reality.

For others of my acquaintance, an eye-opening ecumenical experience has occurred initially under quite different circumstances. A period of study at the Ecumenical Institute of the World Council of Churches, at Bossey, Switzerland consistently opens new worlds to those who have been privileged to attend, as does a period of study at the Center for Ecumenical Research at Collegeville, Minnesota. Others have had the privilege of visiting the spiritual retreat center at Taizé, France, and have been unfailingly moved by its ecumenical depth and breadth. For others, the eye-opening has occurred as an experience of eucharistic hospitality extended by a tradition previously regarded as ecclesiastically alien. For others it has been so simple a thing as attending for the first time a 'Council of Churches' meeting, and being struck by the visual impact of denominational delegates seated in the same room at tables bearing signs which mark their church affiliation.

What is common to all of these experiences, it seems to me, is that it gives a glimpse of the holy catholic Church, even if for but a fleeting moment. The significance of such a glimpse is that it is a kind of epiphany of the Church in its wider dimensions. One has an 'Aha!' experience; and even though it occurs for but an instant, the vision of the Church – one, holy, catholic and apostolic – impresses itself permanently on one's ecclesiological understanding.

The third element in my own ecumenical formation was that of significant mentors whom I was privileged to know or under whom I was privileged to study. Each ecumenist will have his or her own list of those who have been influential in shaping one's ecclesiological orientation. My own list is quite long, and includes pastors, lay persons, seminary professors, and colleagues in ministry. It is my perception that few if any have gained an ecumenical view of the Church and the world on their own. Someone spoke or taught or acted in such a manner as to open up the wider spiritual and ecclesial horizon. That is the essential meaning of ecumenical ministry, whether ordained or lay. I cannot conceive of ecumenical formation without it.

These, then are the three most memorable elements in my own ecumenical formation, up until the time of my initial awareness that I truly cared about the unity of the Church. Since then, my ecumenical understanding has grown in altogether predictable ways: guided study of ecumenical literature, personal relationships with professional colleagues in ecumenical service, involvement in interchurch dialogues, and participation in councils of churches and other institutional expressions of the ecumenical movement. These have immensely enriched my ecumenical experience and understanding; but that which was formative, for me, began much earlier, even in childhood and youth. For me it arose from traditioning, experiencing, and mentoring. That being my story, it influences the way I think about and attempt to exercise my ministry of ecumenical formation with and for others.

PRAYER

O Holy Spirit
who birthed the Church, and dispensed your varied
   gifts for its shared life:
thanks be to you for your gifts that are prized
in that part of Christ's body in which I live;
and if I could, I would praise you as well
for the gifts you have given to others for my sake,
and celebrate with them your sacred bounty in
mutual joy.

But the body is divided;
gifts given for the blessing of us all
are treasured in ways that exclude.
Dear God, for one more gift I pray:
make us one, Lord,
not that we may be strong
but that we may be dependent on you
through the fullness of your gifts
for the common good.

Sentences for discussion

Spiritual ecumenism
Ecumenical formation in my view is a subcategory of spiritual formation. It has little to do with ecclesiastical joinery, but with obedience to Christ's will for the Church.

The wider vision
I was privileged to attend a conference of the Student Volunteer Movement held at Wooster, Ohio in December, 1943. The impact of such an event is greater than the content of the speeches, all soon forgotten. What such an event does is open up for the participant a wider vision of the holy catholic Church – which is the essence of the ecumenical reality.

Ecumenical ecclesiology
A thorough traditioning in the doctrine and discipline of any of the mainline Christian denominations will include some attention to the history, doctrine, worship, and polity of the Church – that is to say 'ecclesiology'. In my view, there is no such thing as an ecumenist who does not care deeply about these things. That is what most distinguishes ecumenical Christianity from individualistic, subjectivistic forms of popular religiosity.

Traditions
I have never met an identifiable ecumenist who was not

also and at the same time a deeply committed participant in his or her own particular church tradition.

Ecumenical apostolate

It is my perception that few if any have gained an ecumenical view of the Church and the world on their own. Someone spoke or taught or acted in such a manner as to open up the wider spiritual and ecclesial horizon. That is the essential meaning of ecumenical ministry, whether ordained or lay. I cannot conceive of ecumenical formation without it.

J. M. R. Tillard

OP (Dominican), Collège dominicain, Ottawa, Canada. Member of the First and Second Anglican-Roman Catholic International Commissions, Vice-Moderator of the Faith and Order Commission, World Council of Churches. *Roman Catholic.*

Translated from the French by Joan Greatrex,
Robinson College, Cambridge.

It is always difficult to pinpoint the precise moments when God's grace has intervened in our lives and left behind his imprint. Whenever I hear or read the self-assured remarks of those who claim that in such and such a place at such and such a time they have had an encounter with God, I invariably ask myself 'surely there must be a large measure of illusion here?' For, who can possibly identify a reality which is altogether mysterious and complex, and is utterly hidden in the innermost depth of our being? God's encounters with us are his own secret which it would be blasphemous to claim to have penetrated.

I intend, therefore, to speak of significant events, rather than of decisive moments in my personal experience. These take me back to the earliest days of my ecumenical involvement in the wake of the Second Vatican Council, in which I was one of the participating theologians, an involvement which became clearly defined by my presence at the Uppsala Assembly in 1968. Among these major events I would place the unforgettable gathering of the members of ARCIC I[1] on their final evening at Windsor. It was 3 September, 1981, and what an evening it turned out to be! Against the background of rain and cold outside the two co-Chairmen followed up our approval of the Final Report by putting before us an important decision that had been proposed, namely, that since we had fulfilled our mandate it was time to submit our resignations to the two authorities concerned, Rome and Canterbury. Although some members, of whom I was the first to respond, produced objections, the majority considered this to be the right decision. Our celebration of the approval of *The Final Report* then continued, and it turned into a prolonged celebration tinged with nostalgia, as we lingered on together for the last time, unwilling to depart despite the coldness of the library.

This was the final chapter of what I would describe as a 'marvellous adventure' which had begun eleven years earlier, in 1970, in that same library. On the earlier occasion, when we had found ourselves together on the first evening, there were two clearly distinguishable groups, strangers to one another, behaving politely but somewhat cautiously, each group conscious of its position and clutching its inheritance of a more or less instinctive mistrust of the other. One of the Anglicans, whom I had previously met at the Council and who now kindly came forward to introduce me to his colleagues, made a good humoured reference to this situation when he pointed out one of them seated at the other end of the table: 'watch this clergyman; he is an evangelical and he will be the Ottaviani of this commission'. The evangelical was Julian Charley.

By the end of this, our first meeting, Julian and I were both surprised to discover that a broad consensus of agreement on essentials had already become evident. This initial mutual understanding blossomed into a close friendship. When I was later invited to lecture at St John's College in Nottingham – an occurrence which in itself provoked in some quarters a gnashing of teeth and venting of spleen! – I encountered a richness of evangelical life and pastoral gifts which made a lasting impression on me. Working together over a lengthy period of patient reflection and exacting research, he and I prepared the drafts of the texts that had been assigned to us; and in the final wording it is impossible to pick out which phrases were his and which were mine.

When I recall Bishop Butler pausing for a moment during the act of filling his pipe to speak (alluding to Julian and myself) of the 'miracle of the *conciliatio contradictorium*'.[3] I do so not merely because I have been asked to speak of my own experience but also, and more importantly, because my experience of the years of ARCIC I has been the common experience, though perceived and expressed in different ways, of all the members, of the commission. In other words we found that we were sharing in a remarkable experience, that of the *koinonia* which was our goal. Not the kind of 'kissy-kissy and smiling unity' (to use a once popular expression of mine) but a real communion of minds and hearts as we grew more open and responsive to one another through our often formidable study sessions, and began to acknowledge our common awareness of all that united us in one and the same faith, one and the same love of God's Church.

There were annual meetings of a subcommission at the home of Bishop Alan Clark (the Catholic co-chairman) at Poringland, where the only cloud on the horizon for me was the Bishop's cruel declaration of war on an army of rabbits whom he had accused of invading his cabbage patch. Our sessions were dedicated to study but not lacking in lively discussion, and there was no trace of the kind of search for a unity based on 'the lowest common denominator'. At one point, quite often, Bishop Butler forcefully uttered *non possumus*[5] when, after two days spent in discussion of a new text prepared by Julian and me, or of the return to patristic sources, its acceptance was proposed by the 'Gallican mafia' (Duprey, Tavard, Tillard). From the other side Bishop Henry McAdoo (Anglican co-chairman) did not hesitate to declare 'this is a partial statement' when he felt that the tradition of the Anglican Divines had been impugned by his own colleagues. One of the signs of our finding ourselves drawn together in communion was that it was often an Anglican (Henry Chadwick, Bishop Knapp-Fisher) who reminded the Catholics of the interpretation of a point having its source in the thought of the Council of Trent which they had neglected to mention. In their turn the Catholics were able to provide the Anglicans with insights into the richness of their own tradition.

The meetings were often tense, not because of any problems in personal relations, but because of the complexities surrounding points of doctrine, all aspects of which had to be subjected to investigation. These days often proved gruelling, especially when, at the last minute, an objection was raised which required us to go back to the starting point and begin all over again. (One of the members whom I named 'our St Jude, advocate of lost causes' had the knack of referring us to Denzinger[4] just as we were looking forward to the well-earned glass of whisky.)

Finally, there were sessions for which long hours of concentrated study were the prerequisite and during which frustration was an all too common experience when our arduously written pages were whittled down to a few lines and in the final text were reduced to a few words. We expected even these to disappear under the scrutiny of the full Commission. But throughout these times of travail and joy there was a forging of communion.

Herein lies the explanation for the fact that, when the full Commission assembled, the discussions were able to go straight to the central issues. The two co-chairmen (Bishops Clark and McAdoo) did not permit any irrelevant exchanges to divert us from our task; and, even when Howard Root or Bishop Felix Arnott interjected a humorous comment, our relaxation had lasted no longer than two puffs of the pipe before we were called to resume work by the often repeated 'please, let us work, please let us finish this paragraph before the break'. (The Commission had much in common with a club of pipe smokers.)

In truth, our sole preoccupation was the goal of unity, a unity which together we were already experiencing, and not merely at the level of the frankness and friendship which we all enjoyed. It was evident also in a mutual concern for one another that was exemplified by Herbert Ryan who was always attentive to every need, no matter how slight, especially of the older members. Underlying our relationship with one another was our profound conviction of a unity in faith and in the one Church of God to which we belonged, a unity which had developed among us all as a consequence of our research and discussions (with the possible exception of one member of the group).

Thus, as a Commission we found ourselves living and experiencing the tragic drama of our two churches, unable to share the same Eucharist Table, unable to pronounce ourselves canonically 'in communion'; and at the same time we were discovering that our researches – which were conducted according to the most exacting standards of scientific inquiry – had exposed the superficiality of the reasons which continue to be evoked to justify our separate existence. This realization fuelled the intensity of our prayer, a unique experience for me which was unsurpassed even after the Lima Accord on baptism, eucharist and ministry (*BEM*) [5] – prayer both powerful and sublime.

For me, as well as for almost all the members of ARCIC I this was the 'great ecumenical experience'. Since then, it is true that other factors have arisen to wound the harmonious relationship that *The Final Report* had with painstaking perseverance reestablished, two of these being the ordination of women to the Anglican episcopate and the icy breeze circulated by the Vatican response to *The Final Report*, which has withered the budding sprigs of hope. Nevertheless – to speak for myself as I have been requested – if I retain hope for ecumenism in my heart it is chiefly due to these remarkable years to which my thoughts constantly return. I visualise again that last evening gathering in the library of Windsor Castle: there were Bishops Moorman, Arnott and Butler (all three now deceased); Ted Yarnold, closing his Denzinger yet again; E. Fairweather, who never once replied to a letter but was able to recall the dates on which they were written; Howard Root, with a vision of Taizé before his eyes; G. Tavard, screening himself from the clouds of smoke billowing around him from seven pipes; A. Vogel, summoning all his resources in order to repeat for the seventh time his argument which had again been omitted from the draft; H. McAdoo, once more taking up the defence of his solution to the problem of mixed marriages; H. Ryan, bringing for Julian the six Venetian cups which he had wanted; P. Duprey, striding rapidly along the narrow lanes of Venice followed by a flagging troop of Anglicans gasping for breath; W. Purdy, and his distractions; Christopher Hill, and the visits to his modest quarters at Lambeth; Henry Chadwick, with his comments always refreshing and well chosen; Bishop Knapp-Fisher, and his never failing gift for selecting the exact word in our moments of need; Julian.

PRAYER

God, our Father, may Christ's disciples have the grace through your Holy Spirit to discover that the most profound joy within your Church lies in our coming together in one and the same faith and love in order to prepare resolutely for the day when we may share in a common Eucharist.

Why, O Lord, do you stand far off ? Why do you hide yourself in these times of trouble ?

Sentences for discussion

Common life and shared endeavour

I encountered a richness of evangelical life and pastoral gifts which made a lasting impression on me.

Thus, as a Commission we found ourselves living and experiencing the tragic drama of our two churches, unable to share the same Eucharistic Table, unable to pronounce ourselves canonically 'in communion'; and at the same time we were discovering that our researches – which were conducted according to the most exacting standards of scientific enquiry – had exposed the superficiality of the reasons which continue to be invoked to justify our separate existence. This realization fuelled the intensity of our prayer.

Working together over a lengthy period of patient reflection and exacting research, he and I prepared the drafts of the texts that had been assigned to us; and in the final wording it is impossible to pick out which phrases were his and which were mine.

We found that we were sharing in a remarkable experience, that of the *koinonia* which was our goal.

NOTES

1. The first Anglican-Roman Catholic International Commission.

2. The reconciliation of contradictories.

3. 'We can't!'

4. The Enchiridion originally compiled by Denzinger has become a standard condensed handbook of authoritative texts of the Roman Catholic Church.

5. 1982.

Geoffrey Wainwright

A minister of the British Methodist Church, and the Robert E. Cushman Professor of Christian Theology at Duke University, Durham, North Carolina. *Methodist.*

GROWING UP in a Yorkshire village between church and chapel[1] might be a make-or-break experience for a budding ecumenist. In fact, my childhood made me see both the need and the possibility for a reunion between Methodists and Anglicans. My hopes were raised when in 1957 I went up to Cambridge, where Dean Hugh Montefiore welcomed us Nonconformists to the Holy Communion in Caius Chapel and I learned to love Evensong; and where under Arnold Morris's 'high Wesleyan' direction in Methsoc[2] it was unthinkable to be other than friendly in our relations with both the Established[3] and the Free churches. While a student at Cambridge, I was profoundly impressed, during a retreat, by a celebration of the Lord's Supper according to the new rite of the Church of South India, presided over by a missionary presbyter from that church which drew Anglicans, Methodists, Presbyterians and Congregationalists together into a liturgical and ecclesiastical Tradition that reached back further than their separation.

After Cambridge, I trained for the Methodist ministry at Wesley College, Headingley, Leeds (1962–64). Principal Raymond George broadened my ecumenical interests by sending me for a week's intensive study of Eastern Orthodoxy at Bossey, followed by attentive participation in the Holy Week services at the St Serge Institute in Paris. I returned to Bossey for the winter semester at the graduate school and eventually completed the doctorate in theology at the University of Geneva (Calvin's Academy) under the guidance of the Greek Orthodox Nikos Nissiotis (who would become Moderator of Faith and Order of the World Council of Churches). During my time at Bossey, several of us English people responded to the initiative of some

English Benedictines studying at the University of Fribourg (Alban Crossley, Henry Wansbrough, and others), and those contacts founded for me a lasting relationship of affection with that Order.

Before finally sending me out from Headingley, Raymond George took me with him (he said it became his turn every hundred years to nominate a youth delegate) to the meeting of the WCC Faith and Order Commission at Aarhus, Denmark (1964). There I sat with the study group on the Eucharist, whence would eventually emerge the document on Baptism, Eucharist and Ministry, the final redaction of which I guided at Lima, Peru, in January 1982.

After theological college, I was appointed to one of the first partnership churches between Anglicans and Methodists, at Halewood on the outskirts of Liverpool (1964–66). As a young minister I profited from the joint encouragement and example of my Methodist superintendent John Tanner and the Anglican rector Owen Eva.

The year 1966–67 was spent in Rome on a Leverhulme Fellowship. Before Protestant ecclesiastical and academic visitors became ten-a-penny in that city, it was still a special ecumenical privilege to be admitted to the working libraries of the Catholic institutions and to receive invitations to the ordinations of seminarians in the Sistine Chapel. My association with the Waldensian Faculty gave me insight into a long and bitter history, and I learned much from the systematic consistency of the Waldensian dogmatician and ecumenical sceptic Vittorio Subilia. (After almost thirty years, in 1995 I am returning to the Gregorian University in Rome as the McCarthy Visiting Professor in Ecumenical Theology.)

After my Leverhulme year in Rome, I went off to equatorial Africa for six years of missionary service (1967–73), when I taught theology at a united faculty set up in Yaoundé, Cameroon, for university-level theological education among several French-speaking Protestant churches on the West Coast (Presbyterian, Methodist, Lutheran, and Baptist). In the 'ecumenical circle' of Yaoundé and through personal contacts, I came to love the Benedictine community of Mont Febe, and especially its long-serving prior, Father Otmar Bauer from St Gallen, Switzerland.

Back to England, I then taught for six years (1973–79) at the Queen's College in Birmingham, which had recently brought the former Methodist College at Handsworth together with the old Anglican Queen's into what was intended as a model for ecumenical theological education in England. My sense was that, as illustrated in our liturgical life, we were able to retain strong features from our respective traditions while at the same time developing a blend that was more comprehensive than both of us.

In 1979 I moved to the United States, accepting a call as professor of systematic theology at Union Theological Seminary in New York. The four years spent there convinced me that ecumenism was ill-served by an unprincipled pluralism without a firm basis in the classic tradition and a strong center in the living evangelical, catholic, orthodox faith. Since 1983 I have been teaching in the Divinity School and Graduate Program of Duke University (Durham, North Carolina), an institution with Methodist attachments and an ecumenical openness where one's faith commitment is seen less as a handicap to intellectual endeavour than as a proper enabling condition of it.

For fifteen years I served as a member of the Faith and Order Commission of the World Council of Churches and enjoyed the colleagueship and friendship of theologians and ecumenists almost too numerous to mention, although I think especially of Wolfhart Pannenberg, John Zizioulas, Lesslie Newbigin, Jean Tillard, Emmanuel Lanne, Max Thurian, Mary Tanner, Nicholas Lossky, Anton Houtepen ... Then, too, special bonds developed in the four busy years of our collaborations among the team of six that edited the *Dictionary of the Ecumenical Movement*.

While I remain committed to, and engaged in, Faith and Order work (which has benefited from recent geographical and cultural enrichment), I have to confess my concern at some trends within the WCC. My hope is that what General

Secretary Konrad Raiser, in his book *Ecumenism in Transition* (1991), designates as a 'paradigm shift' will turn out to be a temporary hiccough. The hitherto golden years of the twentieth-century ecumenical movement were marked by a Christocentrism and an understanding of the history of salvation, both thoroughly trinitarian, that found theological underpinning and ecclesial expression in the movements for biblical theology, patristic recovery and liturgical renewal. These things are too precious to lose.

In many ways, the manifestation and attainment of ecclesial unity, on the basis of evangelical, catholic, orthodox Christianity, are now best served by the bilateral dialogues that have flourished since Vatican II. Since 1986 I have presided over the World Methodist Council's interest in such dialogues and have chaired the joint commission between the World Methodist Council and the Roman Catholic Church (which has profited on the Catholic side from the presence of George Tavard, Michael Richards, John Onaiyekan and Mary Charles Murray among others) as well as taking part in Methodism's international conversations with the Anglicans and the Orthodox.

My ecumenical hope is that the Western churches, reconciled among themselves, may be sufficiently revived to bring the depth of their common Tradition into the wonderful work which the Triune God is now accomplishing through the Church catholic as it manifests itself in the burgeoning churches of Africa, Asia and the Pacific.

PRAYER

God of endurance and encouragement; give us the
Holy Spirit of truth and love, so that we may with
one heart and one voice glorify you, the God and
Father of our Lord Jesus Christ. Amen.

(after Romans 15.5f)

GEOFFREY WAINWRIGHT

Sentence for discussion

Preserving what is precious
The hitherto golden years of the twentieth-century ecumenical movement were marked by a Christocentrism and
an understanding of the history of salvation, both thoroughly trinitarian, that found theological underpinning
and ecclesial expression in the movements for biblical theology, patristic recovery and liturgical renewal. These things
are too precious to lose.

NOTES

1. In parts of England local communities have for centuries been conscious of a division
between those who belong to the Church of England and 'go to church' and those who
belong to Nonconformist denominations and 'go to chapel'. In the past this often reflected
social patterns.

2. The University's Methodist Society.

3. That is, the Church of England.

Norman Young

Professor of Systematic Theology, United Faculty of Theology, Melbourne, Australia. *Uniting Church in Australia.*

I HAVE BEEN committed to the ecumenical movement for about as long as I have taken the Christian faith seriously – since my late teens. An Australian delegate to the inaugural Assembly of the World Council of Churches (Amsterdam, 1948) came to an interchurch rally in our home town of Geelong, Victoria, and conveyed a vision of Christian people around the world worshipping one Lord, united in one faith and one baptism. That has been an inspiration and guiding light for me ever since.

Two years later I found myself in the Theological College whose principal was that same delegate, Dr Calvert Barber and so his students were constantly challenged to draw implications for Christian unity from our study of the Scriptures, of doctrine and of the history of the Church. It was not surprising, therefore, that soon after I completed my post-graduate study and began teaching theology myself, I became deeply involved in the negotiations for union between the Congregational, Methodist and Presbyterian Churches in Australia, first as a member of the Joint Commission for Union of the three churches, then also as Convener of the Church Union committee of the Methodist Church for the decade leading up to union in 1977.

My ecumenical involvement has taken other forms as well – as a delegate to successive WCC Assemblies, a member for ten years of the Faith and Order Commission, a member of the World Methodist/Roman Catholic International commission since 1975, and currently Chair of the Uniting Church in Australia's Ecumenical Affairs Commission. Rather than continue in anecdotal fashion about these various involvements, however, I have chosen to reflect on the process of negotiation that led up to that union and to draw some conclusions for the wider ecumenical movement.

At an ecumenical summer school held in Melbourne in 1977 Father Duprey reminded those present that genuine ecumenical dialogue is not just an exchange of ideas, in however friendly a fashion, from set positions. It is a process of change, of growing together out of which something new emerges. That is certainly borne out from our experience of the twenty-three years of negotiations that finally culminated in the birth of the Uniting Church in Australia. We also discovered how important was a prior commitment of the federal bodies of all three churches to 'continue with negotiations *until union is achieved*'. That provided the context for all our discussions and sustained us through times of major difficulty, such as the rejection by the churches of the first Basis of Union. It also provided the ground for increasing cooperation at the local level in anticipation of the final union, so that we came together not just in the final act of union but through the long process that led up to it.

From all that, I learned four things in particular which may have significance for the wider ecumenical scene. First, I became aware of the ambiguity of everything in which we became involved. This was not just that in the process we gained some things and lost others, but much more in line with the insight of one of Albert Camus's anti-heroes who affirmed that the shining surface of our best endeavours has its less imposing side. That appears in his novel *The Fall*, and in working for union I discovered again the all-pervasive effect of our sinfulness. Church union is the work both of God and of inevitably sinful and limited human beings, and that affects everything we do.

We hoped, for example, not for the merging of the old but for the emerging of the new, yet many people were won over to the cause of union by being reassured that union would not be all that disturbing. We sought to overcome the scandal of our divisions but caused new disruptions, even the open scandal of former members of the same church going to law against each other over property. We are most concerned for wider unity, but preoccupation with stabilizing our own life has diminished that concern.

None of this is to build a case against union, but to try to put it into the perspective of every endeavour with a human ingredient – it has its less imposing side, but not sufficient to make us wish we had never begun.

Second, the search for unity, if it follows the way of obedience, will follow the way of the Cross. We hope for renewal of the church around living obedience to the way of Christ. However, we must not gauge the genuineness of that renewal by the extent of its popular appeal, for at the heart of the Gospel there lies a true scandal, not the false scandal of our divisions but a genuine and irreducible stumbling block – the proclamation that the way of Jesus is the way of God in the world and the way he calls all people to live. That way of unremitting self-giving love, whose sign is the cross because that is where it led the only one who ever walked it consistently, is an affront to the world, not least to what most in the Australian community hold dear.

Of course Christian unity is a costly business; my point is that that is not unique to Christian unity. It is true of the Christian life itself, and that fact should not be hidden by streamlining structures, updating language or jazzing up worship, because if those reforms succeed in making the Gospel clearer to people then they will at the same time sharpen the scandal. But the world could no longer shrug the scandal off as humbug if the churches were seen more clearly to be at one.

Third, however important and influential the Lund principle has been ('Do separately only those things which for conscience sake we cannot do together') in initiating moves toward unity, it can also be used to put up a Stop sign prematurely. Conscience can be invoked as an alternative to serious reflection, as a way of avoiding the unsettling process of examining cherished presuppositions, and in such a way that no further appeal is allowed. And especially if our conscience has been moulded within our separate denominations without experience of working, talking and praying together, it may be a most unreliable guide to what can and cannot be done together. Appeal to conscience, therefore, is inadequate and misleading unless such conscience is informed, let us say by reason, Scripture, tradition and experience; and unless such experience includes reasoning together, hearing the words of Scripture with, and sharing the insights of tradition alongside our sisters and brothers in Christ who are members of other churches.

Fourth, I have learned again that we must not see our search for unity here in isolation from the rest of the church, militant and triumphant. If we do, we become either arrogant ('Look at what we have achieved') or despairing ('Just look at what we've done'). We are surrounded by a cloud of witnesses to whom we look for encouragement; but also, as the writer to the Hebrews reminds us, who are looking to us for faithfulness. We name before God in gratitude those who set out on the journey toward union and who died on the way, entering the inheritance of the Uniting Church only through us who saw the day of union come. And we pray that our having united will help people in Australia, and in other parts of the world, to believe in the unifying power of the Holy Spirit, and to act upon that belief.

PRAYER

Almighty God, who in Jesus Christ has given us gifts of unity, reconciliation and peace, we pray that those gifts may increasingly be known in the Church;
    that divisions of culture, tradition, denomination, confession
    should no more count in our dealing with each other than they
        do in your dealing with us;
    We acknowledge with shame our failure to distinguish the peripheral from the central,
        preserving our identity as separate churches by stressing our differences,

*refusing to see that the only identity of final worth
is what we share in common, our new creation in
Jesus Christ.*
    *Grant us to manifest our oneness even in our
diversity*
        *that we may become light to the world,
        dispelling rather than reflecting the darkness of its
strife. So may your unity of being-in-community,
Father, Son and Holy Spirit, be echoed in the life of
the Church. Amen.*

Sentences for discussion

Openness to change
Genuine ecumenical dialogue is not just an exchange of
ideas, in however friendly a fashion, from set positions. It
is a process of change, of growing together out of which
something new emerges.

The cost of unity
Of course Christian unity is a costly business; my point is
that that is not unique to Christian unity. It is true of the
Christian life itself, and that fact should not be hidden by
streamlining structures, updating language or jazzing up
worship, because if those reforms succeed in making the
Gospel clearer to people then they will at the same time
sharpen the scandal. But the world could no longer shrug
the scandal off as humbug if the churches were seen more
clearly to be at one.

Perseverance
We discovered how important was a prior commitment of
the federal bodies of all ... churches to 'continue with negotiations *until union is achieved'*.

Practical Applications

Practical Applications

THE STORIES in the preceding chapters are personal, but they show the interrelationship between the personal and institutional dimensions of Christian life. The Vatican II *Decree on Ecumenism* wisely observes that 'There can be no ecumenism worthy of the name without a change of heart.'[1] This reflects the personal dimension of ecumenism. At the same time, because the body of Christ is an incarnate entity which we experience through our churches in all their particularity, the churches also must be involved in this ecumenical enterprise. They are called to manifest fully the unity which Christ has given.

The ecumenical encounters recounted here have occurred for the most part in the context of the churches, and they have implications for the Church. Because the aim of the ecumenical movement is to heal the divisions among churches for the sake of the world, it is appropriate to ask what lessons the churches can learn from this raw data. How can we adjust our ecclesial life to foster ecumenical formation among new generations of leaders? How can we create an ecumenical climate which both stimulates and receives new breakthroughs in the quest for Christian unity?

Churches continue to raise these questions. The new *Directory for the Application of Principles and Norms on Ecumenism*, recently issued by the Vatican's Pontifical Council for Promoting Christian Unity, seriously addresses the challenges of ecumenical formation. The World Council of Churches, in its documents and structures, has long understood that one mark of a good council is its involvement in ecumenical cultivation.

Many of our churches have room for fresh thinking and greater efforts to promote an ecumenical attitude. The personal and the corporate are inextricably intertwined. As Joan Delaney observes, 'When all is said and done, when the structures have been devised and the issues debated, it is the attitudes of people that either move the cause of unity forward or throw up obstacles which make the structure unworkable and the issues unresolvable.' Emmanuel Sullivan suggests that 'We are shaped by the ministries we engage in'. By making a conscious choice to cultivate an ecumenical attitude, and by seeking opportunities to live out the commitment to unity, we may ever more fully reflect a reconciling spirit which informs our church life. Many of our writers are aware that something happened to them which created a climate of openness in which they were able to move more freely than before in their own churches and in the wider church. The editors hope that the following observations will encourage churches and councils of churches to take fresh steps to foster ecumenical formation.

Family life and Christian education
Parental attitudes (positive or negative), neighbourhoods and school environments, Christian education in church youth groups – all these can help set the stage for adult behavior. Churches have special opportunities for ecumenical formation in the development of Christian education curricula for youth and in the attitudes of youth leaders. In fact, our predecessors recognized this, and some of the earliest pan-Protestant ecumenical impulses were in the realm of the Sunday School movement. Some curricula now are developed and used by churches of several traditions. This may, or may not, mean that the Christian unity agenda is consciously included in the curriculum, however, and the development of such curricula provides a good opportunity to address directly the aims of the quest for Christian unity.

The experience of mixed marriages is mentioned as formative by some of the contributors. This is a growing phenomenon, the ecumenical implications of which have not yet been fully explored. Sometimes mixed marriages are viewed by churches more as a problem than as an opportunity. We might benefit by asking, what can we learn from this? To the degree that families find their religious life a stumbling block because of the rubrics of their respective churches, can we enable their pain to remind us about the scandal of the churches' divisions? How can churches help make mixed marriages a positive experience for families, one which enhances our unity? How can we build on these experiences for the good of the ecumenical movement?

Providential encounters and circumstances

David Taylor observes, 'few if any have gained an ecumenical view of the church and the world on their own. Someone spoke or taught or acted in such a manner as to open up the wider spiritual and ecclesial horizon.' Maximilian Mizzi gives an example: 'The meeting with the Anglican Franciscans near the Basilica of St Francis in Assisi, which seemed to be just casual, was the beginning of a very important ecumenical movement in Assisi ... What seemed to be casual proved to be a part of God's plan where Christians belonging to different confessions gather together in love, respect, prayer and reconciliation.' Avery Post describes the same phenomenon: 'I now think of them as bursts – bursting moments after which I would exclaim silently or aloud, 'Now there! There it is!'

We should not underestimate the importance of personal, human encounters in the process of ecumenical transformation. Sometimes, as in the case of Alan Falconer in his youth, the encounter challenges a prejudice and leads to change. If we are open and alert, one thing leads to another. *The churches can foster an environment in which such encounters may occur. They can take seriously the opportunities which ecumenical life now presents* – opportunities such as national or international ecumenical assemblies and educational offerings like those held at the World Council of Churches' Ecumenical Institute at Bossey. Encounters should be more than casual if they are to bear good fruit. They should allow opportunities for conversation to develop understanding and empathy. Since the aims of the ecumenical movement entail change, ecumenical encounters may be anxiety-producing. Thus, the experiences should provide time, space, and means to process feelings as well as information.

Many churches are struggling with finances, and may view ecumenical travel budgets as a luxury. Our writers suggest otherwise. They testify that such encounters often transform lives, and may transform our churches, as well.

You never can tell. Occasionally, an unanticipated ecumenical opportunity presents itself. At such times, we must be ready to seize the day and make as much progress as possible under the circumstances. The ecumenical potential inherent in the Vatican II *Decree on Ecumenism* was such a time. Glenn Hinson speaks of this: 'The timing was providential. Merton once told me that the fall of 1960 was probably the earliest Gethsemani could have permitted classes such as ours to come to Gethsemani.' And Julian Charley says, 'Perhaps some are born ecumenists; some undoubtedly have ecumenism thrust upon them.'

We must be prepared to respond to providence—to be ever vigilant to new opportunities, and take them as far as we are able.

Friends and mentors

Those who have been blessed by them have long been aware of the importance of ecumenical friendships in widening horizons, changing perspectives and nurturing a desire for unity. As Cormac Murphy-O'Connor said, 'Strange, is it not, how a common sense of humour brings people together and this Norman and I had. But beneath it all there was the consciousness of a shared reality of life in Christ ... I found that my meeting and friendship with Norman was the beginning of a new insight into what ecumenism really meant ... Ecumenism is not just "about the removal of obstacles but about the sharing of gifts".'

Churches cannot make this happen. Friendship, in itself, is a gift. Religious leaders can, however, recognize the essential role which friends as mentors play in passing ecumenical expertise from one generation to another, and can assume responsibility for encouraging the sharing of the experiences of more seasoned ecumenists with future leaders. Martin Cressey referred to 'wise senior friends [who] began to teach me that drafting minutes for ecumenical committees is a skilled art.' In fact, by sharing insights he has acquired over years as a behind-the-scenes drafter and master of ecumenical diplomacy, Cressey himself becomes a mentor-in-writing to those who might be called to such tasks in the future.

Charismatic leadership

Some ecumenists stand out and draw others to them. They communicate through their words and their being in ways which invite people to respond. Dean Freiday speaks of ecumenically exemplary individuals. Our churches can be deliberate about identifying such ecumenically charismatic figures, and using them judiciously as speakers, teachers, seminar leaders—wherever their gift of inspiration can excite others about the ecumenical mandate.

The teaching Church

A remarkable number of people mentioned the importance of informed and guided ecumenical exposure during theological college or seminary training as the genesis of their ecumenical involvement. Ecumenical literacy among clergy should begin with seminary education. In too many instances, however, this now occurs through happenstance rather than design. Seminaries and theological colleges could provide, in some relatively simple ways, an organized stimulus to ecumenical awareness. For example, teaching staff who have been privileged to be involved in formal ecumenical life should be recruited to share their experiences in the educational process. Every syllabus should be encouraged to incorporate relevant ecumenical documents. By 'doing theology together', colleges can illustrate the ways in which areas of dispute may be studied ecumenically, to the benefit of all. Teaching staff as well as students should be encouraged to participate in local ecumenical endeavours – not as extracurricular activities, but as essentials in their own continuing education – and should be encouraged to bring their experiences back into the educational process. And seminaries should foster formal instruction in the history, theory and practice of the ecumenical movement.

Dynamics of church structures

Much has been written about the challenging process of 'reception' – of incorporating into the life of our churches official ecumenical actions. All too often, the progress we do make is not known, understood, or used. Churches at every level should be asking, 'To what degree are we helping people appropriate what now is possible?' Churches and councils of churches can hold each other accountable, and push to the limit what is possible in existing agreements.

We must be honest. Not all ecumenical encounters are positive experiences. Sometimes they result in confusion, frustration, and anger. What, as churches, can we do about this phenomenon? How can we help people learn from their experiences in ways which acknowledge occasional frustrations and promote genuine growth?

In both these cases, the role of the experienced ecumenical professional, given recognized authority and adequate resources by his or her church, is essential. Such 'professionals' are able to recognize problems when they surface, to draw on their own skills and the resources of others to defuse difficulties, and to design programs enabling churches imaginatively to maximize official possibilities.

This part of the ecclesial infrastructure now is threatened. Ecumenical staff are easy targets of budget cutters. *With* ecumenical advocates, the process of reception still is difficult, because of the natural resistances of churches to change. *Without* them, the prospects for ecumenical growth may be lessened considerably.

In earlier generations, the World Student Christian Federation was a locus of ecumenical encounters and a training ground for involvement in the Christian unity movement. The World Council of Churches and its conciliar counterparts at other levels of church life potentially serve the same function. One of the marks of a council of churches should be its organized efforts to recruit and cultivate new generations of ecumenical leaders. Councils should be given adequate resources by their members to further this essential aim.

Our contributors also talked about the value of ecumenical structures in places where Christians are threatened, or are in a minority. Günther Gassmann recalled living in a repressive governmental environment, and experiencing the World Council as the one window beyond. He said, 'This was a great consolation and encouragement; we are not alone, we are not finally cut off from the rest of the world, we are part of a community which transcends all political and other barriers.' This is a reminder of the catholicity of the Church, and the importance of understanding that *our* experience does not necessarily encompass the *whole*. In order to comprehend more adequately the church in its fullness, we need opportunities to come together beyond our own boundaries.

Sometimes, representatives of churches attend ecumenical assemblies which give this perspective. On other occasions, ecumenical delegations make local visitations, such as is the custom prior to the General Assembly of the World Council of Churches. Either way, these encounters enflesh the mandate for unity, sometimes in life-changing ways.

Organized efforts for unity
Several contributors spoke of the potentially transforming role of official ecumenical dialogue, both for individual representatives and their churches. Norman Young observes, 'genuine ecumenical dialogue is not just an exchange of ideas, in however a friendly a fashion, from set positions. It is a process of change, of growing together out of which something new emerges.' Aram Keshishian makes a similar point: 'ecumenism is an *existential dialogue* ... It is a

dialogue of people before being a dialogue of ideas, views, perspectives. When the people come together, to think together and to pray together, through that dialogical togetherness, histories, traditions and theologies enter into a dynamic process of creative inter-action, which is in fact a source of enrichment and mutual growth.' Jean Tillard graphically describes this process of transformation: 'Thus, as a Commission we found ourselves living and experiencing the tragic drama of our two Churches, unable to share the same Eucharistic Table, unable to pronounce ourselves canonically in communion; and at the same time we were discovering that our researches – which were conducted according to the most exacting standards of scientific inquiry – had exposed the superficiality of the reasons which continue to be invoked to justify our separate existence. This realization fuelled the intensity of our prayer ...'

These testimonies illustrate the power, the pain, and the potential of dialogue. People feel a certain awkwardness, suspicion, and anxiety about that which is unfamiliar. One of the perennial challenges of the ecumenical movement is that it constantly draws us into the unfamiliar, the foreign. It stretches our boundaries. The challenge and value of substantive dialogue is that it gives people enough time and space to process new learnings.

Over the years, the ecumenical movement has developed recurring foci for unity such as the Week of Prayer for Christian Unity and the Ecumenical Prayer Cycle. The implementation of these practices can become tired and perfunctory, if we are not careful. On the other hand, they offer regular occasions which people can anticipate, plan for, and use to make the aims of ecumenism real in local contexts. With a little imagination and energy, simple practices can grow over time.

For example, in one area, a council of churches has assumed responsibility for preparing a statement, signed by all religious leaders within the jurisdiction, encouraging participation in the Week of Prayer. The statement has become a vehicle for creating media opportunities in which some of the signers talk about the state of ecumenical life in their region. These two practices have led to a third initiative – the encouragement by them of ecumenical Bible study on the theme of the Week of Prayer. In this way, annual Week of Prayer services, which sometimes were problematic because they did not engage people to share with each other in any meaningful way, have become the occasion for deeper sharing.

Conclusion

Our contributors have testified that the call to unity is *rooted in the very being of the God we know in Jesus Christ through the Holy Spirit*. David Taylor says, 'Ecumenical formation in my view is a subcategory of spiritual formation. It has little to do with ecclesiastical joinery, but with obedience to Christ's will for the Church.' Julian Charley says, 'It's all a matter of obedience to Jesus Christ.' And Metropolitan Mar Gregorios says, 'If the movement is really from God it will soon find its own direction.'

In some cases our contributors described an 'aha' experience – a memorable moment or event. In others, the encounters were part of a gradual awakening. The initial impetus usually was the beginning of a process which required patience and persistence. William Rusch speaks to this: 'most ecumenically committed individuals are products of long processes of development and interaction. Rarely does one experience, one person or one event an ecumenist make!'

We respond to the ecumenical mandate in very personal ways, but we do so in the context of the Church. Thus, all these personal stories, whether short bursts of insight or gradual processes of development, have underscored the importance of structures which sustain.

The stories also have highlighted the value of ecumenical witnessing. The stuff of the Christian unity movement, of necessity, involves careful, exacting theological and diplomatic dialogue and negotiation at the highest levels of ecclesial life. But it also requires energy and excitement which come from ecumenical encounters experienced and shared.

We encourage our readers to seek such opportunities. We pray that you will be enriched by them. We urge you to share them. In these ways, all of us can respond to the call to unity.

NOTE
1. Chapter II, par. 7.

List of Contributors

Douglas Brown, SSM (Society of the Sacred Mission), Director of The Anglican Centre in Rome. *Anglican.*

Margrethe B. J. Brown, formerly Associate of the New York State Council of Churches, New York, NY, USA. *Presbyterian Church (USA).*

Edward Idris Cassidy, Cardinal, and President of the Pontifical Council for Promoting Christian Unity. *Roman Catholic.*

Julian Charley, Member of the First and Second Anglican-Roman Catholic International Commissions (1970–91). *Anglican.*

Choan-Seng-Song, Professor of Theology and Asian Cultures, Pacific School of Religion and member of the Doctoral Faculty of the Graduate Theological Union in Berkeley, California. *Reformed.*

Martin H. Cressey, Principal of Westminster College, Cambridge, England. *United Reformed Church*

Paul A. Crow, President of the Council on Christian Unity of the Disciples of Christ, Vice-Moderator of the Faith and Order Commission, World Council of Churches, and Editor of the Journal Midstream. *Disciples of Christ.*

Joan Delaney, MM (Maryknoll Missioner), Director of Mission Research at the Maryknoll Sisters Center in New York, USA. *Roman Catholic.*

Alan D. Falconer, Formerly Director of the Irish School of Ecumenics; Director of the Faith and Order Commission Secretariat, World Council of Churches. *Reformed.*

Kyriaki Karidoyanes Fitzgerald, Theologian, serving on the Faith and Order Commission of the World Council of Churches, representing the Ecumenical Patriarch of Constantinople. *Eastern Orthodox.*

Dean Freiday, member and past clerk of the Christian and Interfaith Relations Committee of Friends General Conference, Philadelphia, USA. *Religious Society of Friends.*

Günther Gassmann, formerly Director of the Commission on Faith and Order of the World Council of Churches (1987–94). *Lutheran.*

Paulos Mar Gregorios, Metropolitan of Delhi, President Inter-Religious Federation for World Peace, New York, USA. Former President, World Council of Churches. *Oriental Orthodox.*

Stanley Samuel Harakas, Archbishop Iakovos Professor of Orthodox Theology, Holy Cross Greek Orthodox School of Theology, Brookline, Massachusetts, USA. *Eastern Orthodox.*

Christopher Hill, Canon Precentor of St Paul's Cathedral, London, England. Formerly Secretary for Ecumenical Affairs to the Archbishop of Canterbury. *Anglican.*

E. Glenn Hinson, John Loftis Professor of Church History, Richmond Theological Seminary, Richmond, Virginia, USA. *Southern Baptist.*

Rena Karefa-Smart, Ecumenical Officer, Episcopal Church USA, Diocese of Washington, DC. *African Methodist Episcopal Zion and Episcopal.*

Aram Keshishian, Primate of the Armenian Orthodox Church in Lebanon and Moderator of the Central Committee of the World Council of Churches. *Oriental Orthodox.*

Harding Meyer, retired, Centre d'Études Oecuméniques, Strasbourg, France. *Lutheran.*

Maximilian Mizzi, Delegate General for Ecumenism and Interreligious Dialogue, Friars Minor Conventual. Founder of the Franciscan International Centre for Dialogue, Assisi, Italy. *Roman Catholic.*

Walter G. Muelder, Dean and Professor of Social Ethics, Emeritus, Boston University School of Theology, Boston, Massachusetts, USA. *United Methodist.*

Cormac Murphy O'Connor, Bishop of Arundel and Brighton, England, and Roman Catholic Co-Chairman of ARCIC II. *Roman Catholic.*

William A. Norgren, retired Ecumenical Officer, The Episcopal Church in the United States of America, New York, NY, USA. *Anglican.*

Mercy Amba Oduyoye, Deputy General Secretary, World Council of Churches. *Methodist.*

Ofelia Ortega, Executive Director, Programme on Theological Education of the World Council of Churches for Latin America and the Caribbean. *Presbyterian-Reformed.*

John S. Pobee, Co-ordinator of Ecumenical Theological Education of Unit I on Unity and Renewal, World Council of Churches. Member of the Second Anglican-Roman Catholic International Commission. *Anglican.*

Avery D. Post, former President, United Church of Christ and former member of the Central Committee of the World Council of Churches. *United Church of Christ.*

Brother Roger of Taizé, founder and leader of the ecumenical Community of Taizé, France. *Reformed.*

William G. Rusch, Director of the Department for Ecumenical Affairs and Assistant to the Bishop, Evangelical Lutheran Church in America, Chicago, USA. *Lutheran.*

Turid Karlsen Seim, Member of the International Roman Catholic-Lutheran Dialogue, Professor of Theology (New Testament) and Dean of the Faculty of Theology, University of Oslo, Norway. *Lutheran.*

Krister Stendhal, Bishop of Stockholm, Sweden (retired). *Lutheran.*

Emmanuel Sullivan, SA (Franciscan Friar of the Atonement), Episcopal Vicar for Ecumenical Affairs, Diocese of Arundel and Brighton and member of the Committee for Christian Unity of the Catholic Bishops' Conference of England and Wales. *Roman Catholic.*

Mary Tanner, Moderator of the Faith and Order Commission, World Council of Churches, General Secretary of the Council for Christian Unity, of the General Synod of the Church of England. *Anglican.*

David W. A. Taylor, former General Secretary of the Consultation on Church Union, Princeton, New Jersey, USA. *Presbyterian.*

Jean Tillard, OP (Dominican), Collège dominicain, Ottawa, Canada. Member of the First and Second Anglican-Roman Catholic International Commissions, and of the Orthodox-Roman Catholic International Commission; Vice-Moderator of the Faith and Order Commission, World Council of Churches. *Roman Catholic.*

Geoffrey Wainwright, Minister of the British Methodist Church, and the Robert E. Cushman Professor of Christian Theology at Duke University, Durham, North Carolina, USA. *Methodist.*

Norman Young, Professor of Systematic Theology, United Faculty of Theology, Melbourne, Australia. *Uniting Church in Australia.*

Index

ecumenical formation iv
El Salvador 26
empathy 55
Episcopalians (see Anglicans)
Eucharist 131, 167, 187
Evangelicals 7, 59
Evanston, 1954 12
Fairweather, E. 200
Faith and Order 11, 36, 37ff., 51,
71, 130, 203-5
Falconer, Alan 5, 217
Florence, Council of 8
Florovsky, G. 50
Francis of Assisi 115
Franciscans 114ff., 182ff., 217
Freiday, Dean 6, 219
Frere, W. H. 7

Gassmann, Günther 4, 6.221
Gaventa, Beverley 58
Geneva 2, 77, 79, 136, 178, 203
Germany 62, 74, 91
Ghana 139
Goodall, Norma, 125
Gore, C. 7
Greece 8, 162
Gregorios, Paulos Mar 2,7

heaven 126
Hebert, Gabriel 15
Heidelberg 74
Hill, Christopher 201
Hindus 56
Hinson, E.Glenn 1,218
history iv
'holy envy' 180
'holy disobedience' 156
Hong Kong 82, 85, 86
Houtepen, Anton 205
Huevel, Albert van den 51
Hungary 174

icons 61
India 129; 144; 187
interfaith dialogue 116
Ireland 182
Itty, C. T. 145ff.

Jesuits 187
Jews 179
John Paul II, Pope 24, 184
John XXIII, Pope 98, 116, 167, 168

Kentucky 49
Keshishian 221
Kidd, B. J. 7
King, Martin Luther 72
kirk 59
Knapp-Fisher, bishop 198, 201

Lambeth 91
Lambeth Conferences 10
Lanne, Emmanuel 205
Laos 117
Latin America 35, 49, 51, 165
Latourette, Kenneth Scott 161
Lausanne 51
Life and Work 10, 11
Lilje, Hanns 48
Lima 187
Liverpool 29
Lord's Table 21
Lossky, Nicholas 205
Lund (1952) 22, 128
Luther, Martin 75
Lutherans 20ff., 51, 74ff., 110,
115, 129, 130, 131, 171, 173ff.

Maeda, Frances 50
Malines 7, 10
Malta 114
Marney, Carlyle 50
McAdoo, H. R. 198, 200
McCord, James I 50
Mel, Laksada de 52
Mercier, D. J., 7
Merton, Thomas 1, 94ff.
Methodists 9, 89, 90, 101ff., 120,
131, 134, 135, 204ff., 208
Mexico City 101
Minear,Paul S. 50
mission 54, 101, 149
Mizzi, Maximilian 1, 2, 217
monasticism 2
Montefiore, Hugh 203

INDEX

Montreal 52
Moorman, bishop 200
Morrison, Charles Clayton 48
Mudge, Lewis 51
Murphy-O'Connor, Cormac 218
Murray, Mary Charles 206
Muslims 56, 137, 139

Nairobi 138
National Councils of Churches 162
New Delhi (1961) 3, 12, 13, 78
New Testament 72
New York 129
New Zealand 138
Newbigin, 205
Newbigin, Lesslie 52
Niebuhr, Richard 77, 161
Nigeria 139
Nikodim, Metropolitan 51
Niles, D. T. 48
Nissiotis, Nikos 51, 60, 203
Northern Ireland 55
Norway 173
Norways 173

Oberlin 50
Oduyoye, Mercy Amba 153
Ohio 50
Onaiyekan, John 206
Orange Lodges 29
Orthodox 2, 8, 17, 51, 61-2.65ff., 77ff., 97, 130, 131, 173, 180, 206
Osbord, Ronald E. 50
Ottaviani 197
Ottawa 39
Outler, Albert C. 50
Oxford 75, 78

Pacific 35
Pakistan 129
Pannenberg, Wolfhart 205
Pentecostals 97, 173, 180
Peru 187
pilgrimage 167
pluralism 152, 160
Pobee, John 6

Pontifical Council for Christian Unity 146
Potter, Philip 48, 163
poverty 166
prayer 108
Presbyterians 42, 135, 145, 191, 208
Princeton 77
protestants 77, 83, 84, 130, 180
Purdy, William 201

Quakers, see Society of Friends

Raiser, Konrad 206
Ramsay, Michael 52
Ramsey, Ian 88
Reformed 51, 125
Reformed Churches, World Alliance of 43, 59
Reid, J. K .S. 59
Robinson, J. A. 7
Roman Catholic
Roman Catholic Church 8, 9, 10, 15, 28, 59, 60, 61, 88, 90, 110ff., 128, 134, 155, 173ff., 182
Rome 204
Root, Howard 200
Runcie, Robert 91
Rusch, W. 6
Russia 97
Ryan, H., 200

sacrifice 67
Salvation Army 72
salvation 67
Santago de Compostela 138
Schmemann, Alexander 50
Schutz, Roger 51
Scotland 52, 59
Seim, Turid Karlsen 1, 5
Sheppard, David 30
Short, Howard E. 49
Sidney 155
Smith, Wilfred Cantwell 179
Society of Friends 70ff.
Society of the Atonement 183
Söderblom, N. 7, 10, 178

233

South Africa 55
Strasbourg 74ff.
Student Christian Federation
   134
Student Christian Movement 9,
   20, 137, 178
Sullivan, Emmanuel 6

Taizé 15, 165ff.
Tamez, Elsa 153
Tanner, Mary 205
Tavard, Georges 198, 200, 206
Taylor, David 1
Tevi, Lorine 153
theological education 32ff., 154ff.,
   219
Thurian, Max 205
Tillard, J, M, R. 2, 7, 198
Tillich, Paul 120
tolerance 185
Tomkins, Oliver 52
Toronto, 1950 12
Trappists 94ff.
Trent, Council of 8
Troeltsch, Ernst 120
Turks 8, 91
Tutu, Desmond 70
Tutu, Leah 153

Uppsala (1968) 79, 138, 196

Vancouver 138
Vancouver (1985) 80
Vatican 117, 146
Vietnam 139
Visser't Hooft, W. A. 50

Wales 42
Week of Prayer for Christian
   Unity 106, 222
Windsor 29
World Council of Churches iii, 2,
   11ff., 35ff., 52, 74 ,77ff. and
   passim
World War I 163
World War II 32,121,161,163
Wyker,Mossie 50

Yale 78
Yarnold, Edward 200
YMCA 82, 121, 149
Young, Andrew 51
Young, Norman 4, 5
YWCA 121, 149

Zikmund, Barbara Brown 153
Zizioulas, John 205